Ninja Woodfire Electric BBQ Grill & Smoker

Cookbook 2024

1900 | Days of Easy & Mouthwatering Grill Recipes to Enjoy with the Family | Including BBQ, Grilling, Bake, Roast, Dehydrate, Broil and More.

Ninja Woodfire Electric BBQ Grill & Smoker

Delisa A. Gordon

All Rights Reserved.

The contents of this book may not be reproduced, copied or transmitted without the direct written permission of the author or publisher. Under no circumstances will the publisher or the author be held responsible or liable for any damage, compensation or pecuniary loss arising directly or indirectly from the information contained in this book.

Legal notice.

This book is protected by copyright. It is intended for personal use only. You may not modify, distribute, sell, use, quote or paraphrase any part or content of this book without the consent of the author or publisher.

Notice Of Disclaimer.

Please note that the information in this document is intended for educational and entertainment purposes only. Every effort has been made to provide accurate, up-to-date, reliable and complete information. No warranty of any kind is declared or implied. The reader acknowledges that the author does not engage in the provision of legal, financial, medical or professional advice. The content in this book has been obtained from a variety of sources. Please consult a licensed professional before attempting any of the techniques described in this book. By reading this document, the reader agrees that in no event shall the author be liable for any direct or indirect damages, including but not limited to errors, omissions or inaccuracies, resulting from the use of the information in this document.

CONTENTS

INTRODUCTION 6

Ninja Woodfire Electric BBQ Grill 7
Seven cooking modes 7
How to cook with Ninja Woodfire Electric Grill? 8
Reasons to recommend Ninja Woodfire Electric BBQ Grill Cookbook 8

Breakfastst 10

Bread Pudding 11
Avocado Quesadillas 11
Veggie Frittata 12
Pesto Egg Croissantwiches 12
Sourdough Croutons 12
Cinnamon Toast With Strawberries 13
Everything Bagel Breakfast Bake 13
Stuffed Bell Peppers With Italian Maple-glazed Sausage 14
Grilled Breakfast Burritos 14
Lush Vegetable Omelet 15
Cornflakes Toast Sticks 15
Blueberry Dump Cake 15
Breakfast Chilaquiles 16
Egg And Bacon Nests 16
Coconut Brown Rice Porridge With Dates 16
Nut And Seed Muffins 17
Chocolate Banana Bread With White Chocolate 17
Banana Churros With Oatmeal 18
Apple And Walnut Muffins 18
Bacon And Broccoli Bread Pudding 19
Pb&j 19
Potato Bread Rolls 20
Grilled Sausage Mix 20
Soufflé 21
Maple Walnut Pancake 21
English Pumpkin Egg Bake 22
Honey-lime Glazed Grilled Fruit Salad 22
Fluffy Pancake Sheet 22

Sides, Snacks & Appetizers 23

Garlic Fries 24
Cheesy Summer Squash With Red Onion 24
Grilled Carrots With Honey Glazed 25
Breaded Green Olives 25
Zucchini And Potato Tots 25
Cajun Zucchini Chips 26
Cheesy Garlic Bread 26
Cheesy Apple Roll-ups 26
Deluxe Cheese Sandwiches 27
Sweet Potato Chips 27
Cheesy Crab Toasts 27
Cheesy Steak Fries 28
French Fries 28
Roasted Mixed Nuts 28
Mushroom And Spinach Calzones 29
Sausage And Mushroom Empanadas 29
Cuban Sandwiches 30
Grilled Shishito Peppers 30
Queso Bomb 30
Mozzarella Sticks 31
Spicy Kale Chips 31
Blistered Lemony Green Beans 31
Dill Pickles 32
Creamy Artichoke Dip With Pita Chips 32
Homemade Bbq Chicken Pizza 33
Crispy Cod Fingers 33
Rosemary Baked Cashews 33
Jalapeño Poppers 34
Bacon-wrapped Dates 34
Brussels Sprouts And Bacon 34
Twice Air-crisped Potatoes 35

BBQ Grill & Smoker Cookbook

Bacon-wrapped Onion Rings And Spicy Aioli 35

Meatless 36

Cheesy Asparagus And Potato Platter..................37
Stuffed Squash With Tomatoes And Poblano 37
Summer Squash And Zucchini Salad...................38
Honey-glazed Roasted Veggies............................38
Asian-inspired Broccoli......................................39
Cheesy Broccoli Gratin......................................39
Prosciutto Mini Mushroom Pizza 39
Flatbread Pizza..40
Loaded Zucchini Boats......................................40
Honey-glazed Baby Carrots................................40
Mozzarella Broccoli Calzones 41
Mascarpone Mushrooms....................................41
Crispy Noodle Vegetable Stir-fry........................42
Sriracha Golden Cauliflower..............................42
Bean And Corn Stuffed Peppers 43
Grilled Vegetable Quesadillas............................43
Crusted Brussels Sprouts With Sage...................44
Fast And Easy Asparagus...................................44
Spicy Cauliflower Roast 44
Black Bean And Tomato Chili 45
Cheesy Macaroni Balls 45
Simple Ratatouille...45
Vegetarian Meatballs...46
Hearty Roasted Veggie Salad 46
Creamy Corn Casserole 47
Corn Pakodas 47
Garlic Roasted Asparagus...................................47
Grilled Mozzarella And Tomatoes 48
Cashew Stuffed Mushrooms..............................48
Creamy And Cheesy Spinach............................48

Meats 49

Garlic Herb Crusted Lamb................................50
Spaghetti Squash Lasagna..................................50
Bacon-wrapped Scallops....................................51
Spicy Pork With Candy Onions.........................51
Cheesy Beef Meatballs 51
Sweet And Tangy Beef.......................................52
Spicy Beef Lettuce Wraps..................................52
Carne Asada Tacos..53
Crispy Pork Tenderloin 53
Herb And Pesto Stuffed Pork Loin.....................54
Bacon Burger Meatballs.....................................54
Teriyaki Pork And Mushroom Rolls 55
Vietnamese Pork Chops 55
Barbecue Pork Ribs...55
Rack Of Lamb Chops With Rosemary................56
Smoked Beef...56
Homemade Teriyaki Pork Ribs 56
Citrus Carnitas 57
Italian Sausage And Peppers..............................57
Mozzarella Meatball Sandwiches With Basil 57
Pork Sausage With Cauliflower Mash 58
Easy Beef Schnitzel 58
Lamb Ribs With Fresh Mint 58
Uncle's Famous Tri-tip 59
Apple-glazed Pork...59
Grilled Pork Banh Mi..60
Pork Chops In Bourbon 60
Golden Wasabi Spam 61
Potato And Prosciutto Salad...............................61
Crackling Pork Roast 61

Sauces, Dips, And Dressings....................62

Garlic Lime Tahini Dressing..............................63
Ginger Sweet Sauce 63
Lemon Dijon Vinaigrette 63
Creamy Ranch Dressing 63
Pico De Gallo..64
Cashew Vodka Sauce 64
Balsamic Dressing 64
Hummus...64
Cashew Pesto 65
Cashew Ranch Dressing 65

Poultry 66

Lemon Parmesan Chicken 67

Pecan-crusted Turkey Cutlets 67
Salsa Verde Chicken Enchiladas 68
Grilled Turkey Pesto Sandwiches 68
Buttermilk Ranch Chicken Tenders 69
Sweet Chili Turkey Kebabs 69
Chicken Cordon Bleu Roll-ups 70
Ginger Chicken Thighs 70
Deep Fried Duck Leg Quarters 71
Simple Whole Chicken Bake 71
Teriyaki Chicken And Bell Pepper Kebabs 71
Turkey Meatballs With Cranberry Sauce 72
Adobo Chicken 72
Spicy Chicken Kebabs 73
Lettuce Chicken Tacos With Peanut Sauce 73
Rosemary Turkey Breast 74
Lime-garlic Grilled Chicken 74
Grilled Cornish Hens 75
Crispy Dill Pickle Chicken Wings 75
Lemony Chicken And Veggie Kebabs 76
Garlic Brown-butter Chicken With Tomatoes 76
Crispy Chicken Strips 77
Crispy Chicken Parmigiana 77

Seafood 78

Chili-lime Shrimp Skewers......................................79
Shrimp Boil...79
Grilled Mahi-mahi Tacos With Spicy Coleslaw 80
Honey-walnut Shrimp...80
Crab Cakes With Lemon-garlic Aioli 81
Crusted Codfish...81
Garlic Butter Shrimp Kebabs..................................82
Buttered Lobster Tails 82
Lemon-garlic Butter Scallops 83
Lobster Rolls..83
Coconut Shrimp With Orange Chili Sauce 84
Orange-ginger Soy Salmon....................................84
Striped Bass With Sesame-ginger Scallions 85
Halibut With Lemon And Capers...........................85
Tomato-stuffed Grilled Sole...................................86
Tilapia With Cilantro And Ginger...........................86

Desserts..87

Cinnamon Candied Apples 88
Chocolate Pecan Pie..88
Banana And Walnut Cake 88
Sweet Potato Donuts 89
Fresh Blueberry Cobbler...89
Lemon Squares..90
Everyday Cheesecake 90
Black And White Brownies.....................................91
Lemony Blackberry Crisp..91
Lemon Ricotta Cake 91
Chia Pudding..92
Marshmallow Banana Boat....................................92
Graham Cracker Cheesecake 92
Vanilla Scones..93
Strawberry Pizza 93
Easy Blackberry Cobbler...94
Rum Grilled Pineapple Sundaes 94
Pumpkin Pudding..94
Churros With Chocolate-yogurt Sauce 95
Orange Cake..95
Apple, Peach, And Cranberry Crisp.......................96
Fudge Pie 96
Pound Cake With Mixed Berries 96
Rich Chocolate Cookie 97
Chocolate S'mores 97
Peaches-and-cake Skewers 97
Coffee Chocolate Cake 98
Ultimate Skillet Brownies.......................................98

How can you tackle late night snacking and curb unhealthy choices? 99

Measurement Conversions 100

Appendix: Recipes Index 104

INTRODUCTION

Delisa A. Gordon, whose culinary journey through the smoky fire has earned her the title "Queen of Extraordinary Barbecue." In this tantalizing cookbook, Delisa's passion for barbecue combines with the innovations of the Ninja wood-fired electric grill and smoker for an unparalleled culinary adventure. But first, let's get to the driving force behind these delicious recipes.

Delisa is a true barbecue enthusiast and has been delving into the art of live grilling for years. Her love of grilling began in her grandmother's backyard, where the smoky aroma of charcoal and firewood was a family tradition. Out of culinary curiosity, Delisa began exploring ways to take barbecue cuisine to new heights and embraced the evolution of barbecue technology with the introduction of the Ninja wood-fired electric grill and smoker. As a renowned chef, food writer and advocate of backyard grilling, she combines traditional grilling wisdom with cutting-edge electric grilling innovations.

Delisa's culinary skills are superb as she blends flavors, techniques and ingredients in a mesmerizing dance over an open fire. Her dishes tell the story of backyard gatherings, unforgettable family feasts, and the irresistible allure of perfectly roasted meats and vegetables. Now, she extends an invitation to you, dear reader, to join her in a smoky symphony choreographed by the Ninja Woodfire Electric Grill and Smoker. So fire up your appetite, ignite your curiosity, and prepare to embark on a culinary journey guided by the one and only Delisa A. Gordon, where grilling is an art and the grill itself is a muse.

Ninja Woodfire Electric BBQ Grill

The Ninja Woodfire Electric BBQ Grill is a versatile outdoor cooking appliance that seamlessly combines the convenience of electric grilling with the authentic smoky flavor of a wood-fired grill. This innovative grill features an electric heating element that allows for precise temperature control and even cooking, eliminating the need for propane or charcoal. Its wood chip drawer infuses your dishes with rich, smoky aromas, replicating the traditional barbecue experience. With a spacious cooking surface and multiple cooking zones, it offers versatility for grilling, searing, and smoking a wide range of foods, making it the perfect choice for outdoor enthusiasts and home chefs seeking an authentic wood-fired flavor without the hassle of traditional grills.

Seven cooking modes

Grill: Ideal for steaks, burgers, and vegetables; achieves perfect sear and grill marks.

Sear: Perfect for seafood, chicken breasts, and pork chops; ensures a crispy, caramelized exterior.

Smoke: Great for ribs, brisket, and whole poultry; infuses rich smoky flavor.

Bake: Suitable for pizzas, casseroles, and baked desserts; even and consistent baking.

Roast: Perfect for large cuts of meat, like roasts and whole chickens; ensures even cooking and tender results.

Dehydrate: Ideal for fruits, vegetables, and herbs; preserves nutrients with low-temperature drying.

Broil: Suitable for broiling steaks, fish fillets, and open-faced sandwiches; quick and intense top-down heat for browning.

How to cook with Ninja Wood-fire Electric Grill?

1. Choose a safe, ventilated outdoor location for your Ninja Woodfire Electric Grill. Place the grill on a stable, heat-resistant surface.

2. Use the control panel to select the desired cooking mode (e.g. grill, broil, smoke, bake, roast, dehydrate or sear).

3. Season food with your favorite marinade, rub or spice. Make sure the food is an even thickness for even cooking.

4. Carefully place the seasoned food on the grill. Cover the grill with a lid to keep the heat and smoke consistent.

5. Keep a close eye on the food during cooking, especially when using high temperatures. Depending on your recipe, flip, turn or rotate food as needed to ensure even cooking on both sides.

6. When cooking is complete, remove the food from the grill and let it sit for a few minutes. This will allow the juices to redistribute and make it juicier.

7. Turn off the grill and unplug it. Let the grill cool down. Empty the wood chip drawer and dispose of the ashes.

8. Maintain your Ninja Woodfire Electric Grill regularly by cleaning it after each use and checking for any wear or damage.

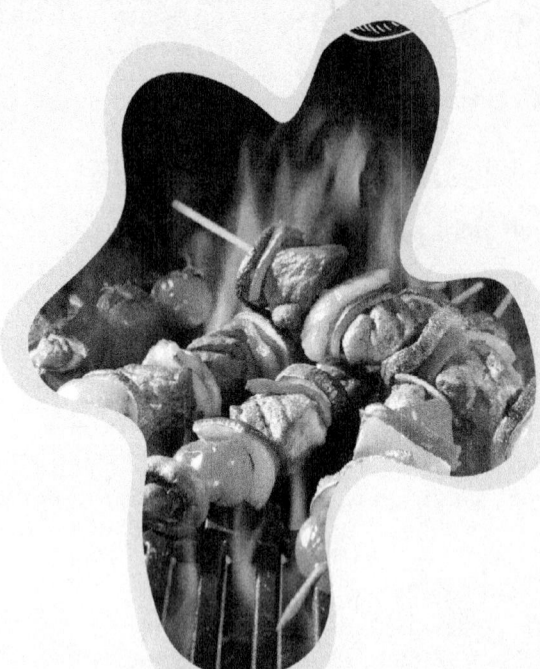

Reasons to recommend Ninja Woodfire Electric BBQ Grill Cookbook

OPTIMIZED FOR THE GRILL

This cookbook is tailor-made for the Ninja Woodfire Electric BBQ Grill, ensuring that all recipes are designed to work seamlessly with this specific appliance, maximizing its potential.

WIDE RANGE OF RECIPES

The cookbook offers a diverse selection of recipes,

from classic barbecue staples to creative and innovative dishes, catering to various tastes and preferences.

COMPREHENSIVE INSTRUCTIONS

Each recipe in the cookbook comes with clear and detailed instructions, making it suitable for both beginners and experienced cooks. You'll find step-by-step guidance for preparing and cooking each dish.

VARIED COOKING MODES

With the Ninja Woodfire Electric BBQ Grill offering multiple cooking modes (Grill, Sear, Smoke, Bake, Roast, Dehydrate, and Broil), this cookbook provides recipes and tips for each mode, ensuring you can make the most of this versatile appliance.

FLAVORFUL RESULTS

The cookbook focuses on helping you achieve mouthwatering and flavorful results. Whether you're after the perfect sear, smoky barbecue flavor, or tender roasts, this cookbook has you covered.

INGREDIENT GUIDANCE

The cookbook offers valuable insights into ingredient selection, helping you choose the best cuts of meat, vegetables, and other components for your recipes.

HEALTHY OPTIONS

For those looking to make healthier choices, the cookbook includes recipes that cater to various dietary preferences, ensuring there's something for everyone.

Breakfastst

BBQ Grill & Smoker
Cookbook

Breakfastst

Bread Pudding

Servings: 6 To 8

Cooking Time: 30 Minutes

Ingredients:

- 1 loaf (about 1 pound) day-old French bread, cut into 1-inch cubes
- 3 large eggs
- 4 tablespoons (½ stick) unsalted butter, melted
- 1 cup milk
- ¾ cup heavy (whipping) cream, divided
- 2 cups granulated sugar, divided
- 1 tablespoon cinnamon
- 1 teaspoon vanilla extract
- 8 ounces cream cheese, at room temperature

Directions:

1. Line the inside bottom and sides of the Cooking Pot with aluminum foil. This will wrap the bread pudding, so make sure it fits the sides of the Cooking Pot.
2. Place the bread cubes in the Cooking Pot.
3. In a large bowl, whisk together the eggs, melted butter, milk, ½ cup of heavy cream, 1 cup of sugar, cinnamon, and vanilla. Evenly pour the mixture over the bread cubes. Place another foil layer on top of the bread cubes, then fold over all the foil ends to seal all around. Place the Cooking Pot in the refrigerator for at least 30 minutes, or overnight, for the bread to absorb the liquid.
4. Insert the Grill Grate and close the hood. Select GRILL, set the temperature to HI, and set the time to 30 minutes. Select START/STOP to begin preheating.
5. While the unit is preheating, prepare your frosting. In a large bowl, whisk together the cream cheese, remaining 1 cup of sugar, and remaining ¼ cup of heavy cream until smooth. Set aside.
6. When the unit beeps to signify it has preheated, place the Cooking Pot with the foil-wrapped bread pudding on top of the Grill Grate. Close the hood and cook for 30 minutes.
7. When cooking is complete, remove the pot from the grill. Use grill mitts to carefully open up the top foil lining. Drizzle the frosting over the bread pudding. Allow the bread pudding to cool before serving.

Avocado Quesadillas

Servings: 4

Cooking Time: 11 Minutes

Ingredients:

- 4 eggs
- 2 tablespoons skim milk
- Salt and ground black pepper, to taste
- Cooking spray
- 4 flour tortillas
- 4 tablespoons salsa
- 2 ounces Cheddar cheese, grated
- ½ small avocado, peeled and thinly sliced

Directions:

1. Select BAKE, set the temperature to 270ºF, and set the time to 8 minutes. Select START/STOP to begin preheating.
2. Beat together the eggs, milk, salt, and pepper.
3. Spray a baking pan lightly with cooking spray and add egg mixture.
4. Place the pan directly in the pot. Close the hood and BAKE for 8 minutes, stirring every 1 to 2 minutes, until eggs are scrambled to the liking. Remove and set aside.
5. Spray one side of each tortilla with cooking spray. Flip over.
6. Divide eggs, salsa, cheese, and avocado among the tortillas, covering only half of each tortilla.
7. Fold each tortilla in half and press down lightly. Increase the temperature of the grill to 390ºF.
8. Put 2 tortillas in Crisper Basket and AIR CRISP for 3 minutes or until cheese melts and outside feels slightly crispy. Repeat with remaining two tortillas.
9. Cut each cooked tortilla into halves. Serve warm.

BBQ Grill & Smoker Cookbook

Veggie Frittata

Servings: 4

Cooking Time: 8 To 12 Minutes

Ingredients:

- ½ cup chopped red bell pepper
- ⅓ cup grated carrot
- ⅓ cup minced onion
- 1 teaspoon olive oil
- 1 egg
- 6 egg whites
- ⅓ cup 2% milk
- 1 tablespoon shredded Parmesan cheese

Directions:

1. Select BAKE, set the temperature to 350ºF, and set the time to 12 minutes. Select START/STOP to begin preheating.
2. Mix together the red bell pepper, carrot, onion, and olive oil in a baking pan and stir to combine.
3. Place the pan directly in the pot. Close the hood and BAKE for 4 to 6 minutes, or until the veggies are soft. Stir once during cooking.
4. Meantime, whisk together the egg, egg whites, and milk in a medium bowl until creamy.
5. When the veggies are done, pour the egg mixture over the top. Scatter with the Parmesan cheese.
6. Bake for an additional 4 to 6 minutes, or until the eggs are set and the top is golden around the edges.
7. Allow the frittata to cool for 5 minutes before slicing and serving.

Pesto Egg Croissantwiches

Servings: 4

Cooking Time: 8 Minutes

Ingredients:

- 4 large eggs
- 4 croissants
- 8 tablespoons pesto

Directions:

1. Insert the Cooking Pot and close the hood. Select GRILL, set the temperature to HI, and set the time to 8 minutes. Select START/STOP to begin preheating.
2. While the unit is preheating, in a small bowl, whisk together the eggs.
3. When the unit beeps to signify it has preheated, pour the beaten eggs into the Cooking Pot. Close the hood and cook for 4 minutes.
4. While the eggs are cooking, split the croissants. Place the croissant halves on top of the Grill Grate.
5. After 4 minutes, open the hood and scramble the eggs with a spatula. Spoon the scrambled eggs onto the bottom halves of the croissants. Remove the Cooking Pot from the unit.
6. Insert the Grill Grate into the unit. Spoon 2 tablespoons of pesto on top of each egg-topped croissant, then top each sandwich with the croissant top. Close the hood and cook for 4 minutes.
7. When cooking is complete, the croissant crust should be toasted. Serve.

Sourdough Croutons

Servings: 4

Cooking Time: 6 Minutes

Ingredients:

- 4 cups cubed sourdough bread, 1-inch cubes
- 1 tablespoon olive oil
- 1 teaspoon fresh thyme leaves
- ¼ teaspoon salt
- Freshly ground black pepper, to taste

Directions:

1. Combine all ingredients in a bowl.
2. Insert the Crisper Basket and close the hood. Select AIR CRISP, set the temperature to 400ºF, and set the time to 6 minutes. Select START/STOP to begin preheating.
3. Toss the bread cubes and transfer to the basket. Close the hood and AIR CRISP for 6 minutes, shaking the basket once or twice while they cook.
4. Serve warm.

Cinnamon Toast With Strawberries

Servings: 4

Cooking Time: 10 Minutes

Ingredients:

- 1 can full-fat coconut milk, refrigerated overnight
- ½ tablespoon powdered sugar
- 1½ teaspoons vanilla extract, divided
- 1 cup halved strawberries
- 1 tablespoon maple syrup, plus more for garnish
- 1 tablespoon brown sugar, divided
- ¾ cup lite coconut milk
- 2 large eggs
- ½ teaspoon ground cinnamon
- 2 tablespoons unsalted butter, at room temperature
- 4 slices challah bread

Directions:

1. Turn the chilled can of full-fat coconut milk upside down (do not shake the can), open the bottom, and pour out the liquid coconut water. Scoop the remaining solid coconut cream into a medium bowl. Using an electric hand mixer, whip the cream for 3 to 5 minutes, until soft peaks form.
2. Add the powdered sugar and ½ teaspoon of the vanilla to the coconut cream, and whip it again until creamy. Place the bowl in the refrigerator.
3. Insert the Grill Grate and close the hood. Select GRILL, set the temperature to MAX, and set the time to 15 minutes. Select START/STOP to begin preheating.
4. While the unit is preheating, combine the strawberries with the maple syrup and toss to coat evenly. Sprinkle evenly with ½ tablespoon of the brown sugar.
5. In a large shallow bowl, whisk together the lite coconut milk, eggs, the remaining 1 teaspoon of vanilla, and cinnamon.
6. When the unit beeps to signify it has preheated, place the strawberries on the Grill Grate. Gently press the fruit down to maximize grill marks. Close the hood and GRILL for 4 minutes without flipping.
7. Meanwhile, butter each slice of bread on both sides. Place one slice in the egg mixture and let it soak for 1 minute. Flip the slice over and soak it for another minute. Repeat with the remaining bread slices. Sprinkle each side of the toast with the remaining ½ tablespoon of brown sugar.
8. After 4 minutes, remove the strawberries from the grill and set aside. Decrease the temperature to HIGH. Place the bread on the Grill Grate; close the hood and GRILL for 4 to 6 minutes until golden and caramelized. Check often to ensure desired doneness.
9. Place the toast on a plate and top with the strawberries and whipped coconut cream. Drizzle with maple syrup, if desired.

Everything Bagel Breakfast Bake

Servings: 4

Cooking Time: 25 Minutes

Ingredients:

- 6 large eggs
- 2 cups milk
- ½ cup heavy (whipping) cream
- 4 everything bagels, cut into 1-inch cubes (or bagel flavor of choice)
- 2 cups cherry tomatoes
- 1 pound cream cheese, cut into cubes

Directions:

1. In a large bowl, whisk together the eggs, milk, and heavy cream.
2. Add the bagel cubes to the egg mixture. Set aside to rest for 25 minutes.
3. After 25 minutes, insert the Cooking Pot and close the hood. Select BAKE, set the temperature to 375°F, and set the time to 25 minutes. Select START/STOP to begin preheating.
4. While the unit is preheating, slice the cherry tomatoes into thirds.
5. When the unit beeps to signify it has preheated, pour the bagel mixture into the Cooking Pot. Top with the sliced cherry tomatoes and evenly place the cream cheese cubes over the top. Close the hood and bake for 25 minutes.
6. When cooking is complete, remove the pot from the grill and serve.

Stuffed Bell Peppers With Italian Maple-glazed Sausage

Servings: 6

Cooking Time: 28 Minutes

Ingredients:

- 2 pounds ground Italian sausage or links
- 1 cup light brown sugar, packed
- 6 bell peppers (any color)
- 1 cup water
- 12 tablespoons (¾ cup) maple syrup, divided

Directions:

1. Insert the Cooking Pot and close the hood. Select GRILL, set the temperature to HI, and set the time to 8 minutes. Select START/STOP to begin preheating.
2. While the unit is preheating, remove the sausage from the casings if using links.
3. When the unit beeps to signify it has preheated, place the sausage and brown sugar in the Cooking Pot. Use a wooden spoon or potato masher to break the sausage apart and mix it with the brown sugar. Close the hood and cook for 8 minutes.
4. While the sausage is cooking, cut the top off each bell pepper and remove the seeds. Then slice the bell peppers in half lengthwise.
5. When cooking is complete, spoon the sausage into each bell pepper cup. Add the water to the Cooking Pot. Place 6 bell pepper halves on the Grill Grate, and place the Grill Grate in the unit.
6. Select GRILL, set the temperature to HI, and set the time to 20 minutes. Select START/STOP and then press the PREHEAT button to skip preheating. Close the hood and cook for 5 minutes.
7. After 5 minutes, open the hood and drizzle 1 tablespoon of maple syrup in each bell pepper cup. Close the hood and cook 5 minutes more. After 5 minutes, remove the stuffed peppers and place the remaining 6 stuffed peppers on the Grill Grate. Repeat this step to cook.
8. When cooking is complete, remove the peppers from the grill and serve.
9. Adding raw sausage inside a bell pepper will result in a watery mess.

Grilled Breakfast Burritos

Servings: 4

Cooking Time: 15 Minutes

Ingredients:

- 4 large eggs
- 12 slices bacon, cut into 1-inch pieces
- 1 cup frozen shredded hash browns
- 1 cup shredded Monterey Jack cheese
- 4 (10-inch) flour tortillas
- 2 tablespoons extra-virgin olive oil
- 4 tablespoons sour cream, for topping
- 1 avocado, pitted and diced, for topping

Directions:

1. Insert the Cooking Pot and close the hood. Select AIR CRISP, set the temperature to 390°F, and set the time to 15 minutes. Select START/STOP to begin preheating.
2. While the unit is preheating, in a medium bowl, whisk the eggs. Add the bacon, frozen hash browns, and cheese to the eggs and stir to combine.
3. When the unit beeps to signify it has preheated, pour the egg mixture into the Cooking Pot. Close the hood and cook for 10 minutes.
4. While the eggs are cooking, place the tortillas on top of the Grill Grate.
5. After 10 minutes, open the hood and use a silicone spatula to scramble the eggs and ensure the bacon is cooked. Remove the pot from the unit. Top the center of each tortilla with the scrambled egg mixture. Roll one end of the tortilla over the eggs, fold in the sides, and finish rolling the tortilla. Brush the olive oil over the burritos and place them seam-side down on the Grill Grate. Place the Grill Grate into the unit. Close the hood and cook for the remaining 5 minutes.
6. When cooking is complete, transfer the burritos to plates. Top with the sour cream and avocado and serve.

Lush Vegetable Omelet

Servings: 2

Cooking Time: 13 Minutes

Ingredients:

- 2 teaspoons canola oil
- 4 eggs, whisked
- 3 tablespoons plain milk
- 1 teaspoon melted butter
- 1 red bell pepper, seeded and chopped
- 1 green bell pepper, seeded and chopped
- 1 white onion, finely chopped
- ½ cup baby spinach leaves, roughly chopped
- ½ cup Halloumi cheese, shaved
- Kosher salt and freshly ground black pepper, to taste

Directions:

1. Select BAKE, set the temperature to 350°F, and set the time to 13 minutes. Select START/STOP to begin preheating.
2. Grease a baking pan with canola oil.
3. Put the remaining ingredients in the baking pan and stir well.
4. Place the pan directly in the pot. Close the hood and BAKE for 13 minutes.
5. Serve warm.

Cornflakes Toast Sticks

Servings: 4

Cooking Time: 6 Minutes

Ingredients:

- 2 eggs
- ½ cup milk
- ⅛ teaspoon salt
- ½ teaspoon pure vanilla extract
- ¾ cup crushed cornflakes
- 6 slices sandwich bread, each slice cut into 4 strips
- Maple syrup, for dipping
- Cooking spray

Directions:

1. Insert the Crisper Basket and close the hood. Select AIR CRISP, set the temperature to 390°F, and set the time to 6 minutes. Select START/STOP to begin preheating.
2. In a small bowl, beat together the eggs, milk, salt, and vanilla.
3. Put crushed cornflakes on a plate or in a shallow dish.
4. Dip bread strips in egg mixture, shake off excess, and roll in cornflake crumbs.
5. Spray both sides of bread strips with oil.
6. Put bread strips in Crisper Basket in a single layer.
7. Close the hood and AIR CRISP for 6 minutes or until golden brown.
8. Repeat steps 5 and 6 to AIR CRISP remaining French toast sticks.
9. Serve with maple syrup.

Blueberry Dump Cake

Servings: 6 To 8

Cooking Time: 25 Minutes

Ingredients:

- 3 cups fresh blueberries
- ½ cup granulated sugar
- 1 (16-ounce) box yellow cake mix
- 8 tablespoons (1 stick) unsalted butter, melted

Directions:

1. Select BAKE, set the temperature to 300°F, and set the time to 25 minutes. Select START/STOP to begin preheating.
2. While the unit is preheating, wash and pat dry the blueberries. Then place them and the sugar into the Cooking Pot and mix to coat the fruit with the sugar.
3. In a large bowl, mix together the cake mix and melted butter. Stir until the cake mix is no longer a powder but crumbly like a streusel. Cover the blueberry-sugar mixture with the cake crumble.
4. When the unit beeps to signify it has preheated, place the Cooking Pot in the unit. Close the hood and bake for 25 minutes.
5. Baking is complete when the fresh blueberries have bubbled and the cake crumble is golden brown. Serve.

Breakfast Chilaquiles

Servings: 4

Cooking Time: 15 Minutes

Ingredients:

- 4 cups tortilla chips (40 to 50 chips)
- 1 (10- to 14-ounce) can red chile sauce or enchilada sauce
- 6 large eggs
- ¼ cup diced onion, for garnish
- ½ cup crumbled queso fresco, for garnish
- Chopped fresh cilantro, for garnish

Directions:

1. Select GRILL, set the temperature to HI, and set the time to 15 minutes. Select START/STOP to begin preheating.
2. While the unit is preheating, add the tortilla chips to the Cooking Pot and pour the red chile sauce over them.
3. When the unit beeps to signify it has preheated, place the Cooking Pot in the unit. Crack the eggs, one at a time, over the tortilla chips, making sure they're evenly spread out. Close the hood and cook for 15 minutes.
4. Cooking is complete when the egg whites are firm with a runny yellow center. Garnish with the onion, queso fresco, and fresh cilantro, and serve.

Egg And Bacon Nests

Servings: 12

Cooking Time: 30 Minutes

Ingredients:

- 3 tablespoons avocado oil
- 12 slices bacon
- 12 eggs
- Salt
- Freshly ground black pepper

Directions:

1. Insert the Grill Grate and close the hood. Select GRILL, set the temperature to HI, and set the time to 30 minutes. Select START/STOP to begin preheating.
2. While the unit is preheating, brush the avocado oil in the bottom and on the sides of two 6-cup muffin tins. Wrap a bacon slice around the inside of each muffin cup, then crack an egg into each cup. Season to taste with salt and pepper.
3. When the unit beeps to signify it has preheated, place one muffin tin in the center of the Grill Grate. Close the hood and grill for 15 minutes.
4. After 15 minutes, remove the muffin tin. Place the second muffin tin in the center of the Grill Grate, close the hood, and grill for 15 minutes.
5. Serve immediately or let cool and store in resealable bags in the refrigerator for up to 4 days.

Coconut Brown Rice Porridge With Dates

Servings: 1 Or 2

Cooking Time: 23 Minutes

Ingredients:

- ½ cup cooked brown rice
- 1 cup canned coconut milk
- ¼ cup unsweetened shredded coconut
- ¼ cup packed dark brown sugar
- 4 large Medjool dates, pitted and roughly chopped
- ½ teaspoon kosher salt
- ¼ teaspoon ground cardamom
- Heavy cream, for serving (optional)

Directions:

1. Select BAKE, set the temperature to 375°F, and set the time to 23 minutes. Select START/STOP to begin preheating.
2. Place all the ingredients except the heavy cream in a baking pan and stir until blended.
3. Place the pan directly in the pot. Close the hood and BAKE for 23 minutes until the porridge is thick and creamy. Stir the porridge halfway through the cooking time.
4. Remove from the grill and ladle the porridge into bowls.
5. Serve hot with a drizzle of the cream, if desired.

Nut And Seed Muffins

Servings: 8

Cooking Time: 10 Minutes

Ingredients:

- ½ cup whole-wheat flour, plus 2 tablespoons
- ¼ cup oat bran
- 2 tablespoons flaxseed meal
- ¼ cup brown sugar
- ½ teaspoon baking soda
- ½ teaspoon baking powder
- ¼ teaspoon salt
- ½ teaspoon cinnamon
- ½ cup buttermilk
- 2 tablespoons melted butter
- 1 egg
- ½ teaspoon pure vanilla extract
- ½ cup grated carrots
- ¼ cup chopped pecans
- ¼ cup chopped walnuts
- 1 tablespoon pumpkin seeds
- 1 tablespoon sunflower seeds
- Cooking spray

Directions:

1. Select BAKE, set the temperature to 330ºF, and set the time to 10 minutes. Select START/STOP to begin preheating.
2. In a large bowl, stir together the flour, bran, flaxseed meal, sugar, baking soda, baking powder, salt, and cinnamon.
3. In a medium bowl, beat together the buttermilk, butter, egg, and vanilla. Pour into flour mixture and stir just until dry ingredients moisten. Do not beat.
4. Gently stir in carrots, nuts, and seeds.
5. Double up the foil cups so you have 8 total and spritz with cooking spray.
6. Put 4 foil cups in the pot and divide half the batter among them.
7. Close the hood and BAKE for 10 minutes, or until a toothpick inserted in center comes out clean.
8. Repeat step 7 to bake remaining 4 muffins.
9. Serve warm.

Chocolate Banana Bread With White Chocolate

Servings: 4

Cooking Time: 30 Minutes

Ingredients:

- ¼ cup cocoa powder
- 6 tablespoons plus 2 teaspoons all-purpose flour, divided
- ½ teaspoon kosher salt
- ¼ teaspoon baking soda
- 1½ ripe bananas
- 1 large egg, whisked
- ¼ cup vegetable oil
- ½ cup sugar
- 3 tablespoons buttermilk or plain yogurt (not Greek)
- ½ teaspoon vanilla extract
- 6 tablespoons chopped white chocolate
- 6 tablespoons chopped walnuts

Directions:

1. Select BAKE, set the temperature to 310ºF, and set the time to 30 minutes. Select START/STOP to begin preheating.
2. Mix together the cocoa powder, 6 tablespoons of the flour, salt, and baking soda in a medium bowl.
3. Mash the bananas with a fork in another medium bowl until smooth. Fold in the egg, oil, sugar, buttermilk, and vanilla, and whisk until thoroughly combined. Add the wet mixture to the dry mixture and stir until well incorporated.
4. Combine the white chocolate, walnuts, and the remaining 2 tablespoons of flour in a third bowl and toss to coat. Add this mixture to the batter and stir until well incorporated. Pour the batter into a baking pan and smooth the top with a spatula.
5. Place the pan directly in the pot. Close the hood and BAKE for 30 minutes. Check the bread for doneness: If a toothpick inserted into the center of the bread comes out clean, it's done.
6. Remove from the grill and allow to cool on a wire rack for 10 minutes before serving.

BBQ Grill & Smoker Cookbook

Banana Churros With Oatmeal

Servings: 2

Cooking Time: 15 Minutes

Ingredients:

- For the Churros:
- 1 large yellow banana, peeled, cut in half lengthwise, then cut in half widthwise
- 2 tablespoons whole-wheat pastry flour
- ⅛ teaspoon sea salt
- 2 teaspoons oil (sunflower or melted coconut)
- 1 teaspoon water
- Cooking spray
- 1 tablespoon coconut sugar
- ½ teaspoon cinnamon
- For the Oatmeal:
- ¾ cup rolled oats
- 1½ cups water

Directions:

1. To make the churros
2. Put the 4 banana pieces in a medium-size bowl and add the flour and salt. Stir gently. Add the oil and water. Stir gently until evenly mixed. You may need to press some coating onto the banana pieces.
3. Spray the Crisper Basket with the oil spray. Put the banana pieces in the Crisper Basket and AIR CRISP for 5 minutes. Remove, gently turn over, and AIR CRISP for another 5 minutes or until browned.
4. In a medium bowl, add the coconut sugar and cinnamon and stir to combine. When the banana pieces are nicely browned, spray with the oil and place in the cinnamon-sugar bowl. Toss gently with a spatula to coat the banana pieces with the mixture.
5. To make the oatmeal
6. While the bananas are cooking, make the oatmeal. In a medium pot, bring the oats and water to a boil, then reduce to low heat. Simmer, stirring often, until all the water is absorbed, about 5 minutes. Put the oatmeal into two bowls.
7. Top the oatmeal with the coated banana pieces and serve immediately.

Apple And Walnut Muffins

Servings: 8

Cooking Time: 10 Minutes

Ingredients:

- 1 cup flour
- ⅓ cup sugar
- 1 teaspoon baking powder
- ¼ teaspoon baking soda
- ¼ teaspoon salt
- 1 teaspoon cinnamon
- ¼ teaspoon ginger
- ¼ teaspoon nutmeg
- 1 egg
- 2 tablespoons pancake syrup, plus 2 teaspoons
- 2 tablespoons melted butter, plus 2 teaspoons
- ¾ cup unsweetened applesauce
- ½ teaspoon vanilla extract
- ¼ cup chopped walnuts
- ¼ cup diced apple

Directions:

1. Select BAKE, set the temperature to 330ºF, and set the time to 10 minutes. Select START/STOP to begin preheating.
2. In a large bowl, stir together the flour, sugar, baking powder, baking soda, salt, cinnamon, ginger, and nutmeg.
3. In a small bowl, beat egg until frothy. Add syrup, butter, applesauce, and vanilla and mix well.
4. Pour egg mixture into dry ingredients and stir just until moistened.
5. Gently stir in nuts and diced apple.
6. Divide batter among 8 parchment paper-lined muffin cups.
7. Put 4 muffin cups in the pot. Close the hood and BAKE for 10 minutes.
8. Repeat with remaining 4 muffins or until toothpick inserted in center comes out clean.
9. Serve warm.

Bacon And Broccoli Bread Pudding

Servings: 2 To 4

Cooking Time: 48 Minutes

Ingredients:

- ½ pound thick cut bacon, cut into ¼-inch pieces
- 3 cups brioche bread, cut into ½-inch cubes
- 2 tablespoons butter, melted
- 3 eggs
- 1 cup milk
- ½ teaspoon salt
- Freshly ground black pepper, to taste
- 1 cup frozen broccoli florets, thawed and chopped
- 1½ cups grated Swiss cheese

Directions:

1. Insert the Crisper Basket and close the hood. Select AIR CRISP, set the temperature to 400°F, and set the time to 10 minutes. Select START/STOP to begin preheating.
2. Put the bacon in the basket. Close the hood and AIR CRISP for 8 minutes until crispy, shaking the basket a few times to help it cook evenly. Remove the bacon and set it aside on a paper towel.
3. AIR CRISP the brioche bread cubes for 2 minutes to dry and toast lightly.
4. Butter a cake pan. Combine all the remaining ingredients in a large bowl and toss well. Transfer the mixture to the buttered cake pan, cover with aluminum foil and refrigerate the bread pudding overnight, or for at least 8 hours.
5. Remove the cake pan from the refrigerator an hour before you plan to bake and let it sit on the countertop to come to room temperature.
6. Select BAKE, set the temperature to 330°F, and set the time to 40 minutes. Select START/STOP to begin preheating.
7. Place the covered cake pan directly in the pot. Fold the ends of the aluminum foil over the top of the pan. Close the hood and BAKE for 20 minutes. Remove the foil and bake for an additional 20 minutes. If the top browns a little too much before the custard has set, simply return the foil to the pan. The bread pudding has cooked through when a skewer inserted into the center comes out clean.
8. Serve warm.

Pb&j

Servings: 4

Cooking Time: 6 Minutes

Ingredients:

- ½ cup cornflakes, crushed
- ¼ cup shredded coconut
- 8 slices oat nut bread or any whole-grain, oversize bread
- 6 tablespoons peanut butter
- 2 medium bananas, cut into ½-inch-thick slices
- 6 tablespoons pineapple preserves
- 1 egg, beaten
- Cooking spray

Directions:

1. Insert the Crisper Basket and close the hood. Select AIR CRISP, set the temperature to 360°F, and set the time to 6 minutes. Select START/STOP to begin preheating.
2. In a shallow dish, mix the cornflake crumbs and coconut.
3. For each sandwich, spread one bread slice with 1½ tablespoons of peanut butter. Top with banana slices. Spread another bread slice with 1½ tablespoons of preserves. Combine to make a sandwich.
4. Using a pastry brush, brush top of sandwich lightly with beaten egg. Sprinkle with about 1½ tablespoons of crumb coating, pressing it in to make it stick. Spray with cooking spray.
5. Turn sandwich over and repeat to coat and spray the other side. Place the sandwiches in the Crisper Basket.
6. Close the hood and AIR CRISP for 6 minutes or until coating is golden brown and crispy.
7. Cut the cooked sandwiches in half and serve warm.

Potato Bread Rolls

Servings: 5

Cooking Time: 20 Minutes

Ingredients:

- 5 large potatoes, boiled and mashed
- Salt and ground black pepper, to taste
- ½ teaspoon mustard seeds
- 1 tablespoon olive oil
- 2 small onions, chopped
- 2 sprigs curry leaves
- ½ teaspoon turmeric powder
- 2 green chilis, seeded and chopped
- 1 bunch coriander, chopped
- 8 slices bread, brown sides discarded

Directions:

1. Insert the Crisper Basket and close the hood. Select AIR CRISP, set the temperature to 400°F, and set the time to 15 minutes. Select START/STOP to begin preheating.
2. Put the mashed potatoes in a bowl and sprinkle on salt and pepper. Set to one side.
3. Fry the mustard seeds in olive oil over a medium-low heat in a skillet, stirring continuously, until they sputter.
4. Add the onions and cook until they turn translucent. Add the curry leaves and turmeric powder and stir. Cook for a further 2 minutes until fragrant.
5. Remove the skillet from the heat and combine with the potatoes. Mix in the green chilies and coriander.
6. Wet the bread slightly and drain of any excess liquid.
7. Spoon a small amount of the potato mixture into the center of the bread and enclose the bread around the filling, sealing it entirely. Continue until the rest of the bread and filling is used up. Brush each bread roll with some oil and transfer to the basket.
8. Close the hood and AIR CRISP for 15 minutes, gently shaking the Crisper Basket at the halfway point to ensure each roll is cooked evenly.
9. Serve immediately.

Grilled Sausage Mix

Servings: 4

Cooking Time: 22 Minutes

Ingredients:

- 8 mini bell peppers
- 2 heads radicchio, each cut into 6 wedges
- Canola oil, for brushing
- Sea salt, to taste
- Freshly ground black pepper, to taste
- 6 breakfast sausage links
- 6 hot or sweet Italian sausage links

Directions:

1. Insert the Grill Grate and close the hood. Select GRILL, set the temperature to MAX, and set the time to 22 minutes. Select START/STOP to begin preheating.
2. While the unit is preheating, brush the bell peppers and radicchio with the oil. Season with salt and black pepper.
3. When the unit beeps to signify it has preheated, place the bell peppers and radicchio on the Grill Grate; close the hood and GRILL for 10 minutes, without flipping.
4. Meanwhile, poke the sausages with a fork or knife and brush them with some of the oil.
5. After 10 minutes, remove the vegetables and set aside. Decrease the temperature to LOW. Place the sausages on the Grill Grate; close the hood and GRILL for 6 minutes.
6. Flip the sausages. Close the hood and GRILL for 6 minutes more. Remove the sausages from the Grill Grate.
7. Serve the sausages and vegetables on a large cutting board or serving tray.

BBQ Grill & Smoker Cookbook

Soufflé

Servings: 4

Cooking Time: 22 Minutes

Ingredients:

- ⅓ cup butter, melted
- ¼ cup flour
- 1 cup milk
- 1 ounce sugar
- 4 egg yolks
- 1 teaspoon vanilla extract
- 6 egg whites
- 1 teaspoon cream of tartar
- Cooking spray

Directions:

1. In a bowl, mix the butter and flour until a smooth consistency is achieved.
2. Pour the milk into a saucepan over medium-low heat. Add the sugar and allow to dissolve before raising the heat to boil the milk.
3. Pour in the flour and butter mixture and stir rigorously for 7 minutes to eliminate any lumps. Make sure the mixture thickens. Take off the heat and allow to cool for 15 minutes.
4. Select BAKE, set the temperature to 320°F, and set the time to 15 minutes. Select START/STOP to begin preheating.
5. Spritz 6 soufflé dishes with cooking spray.
6. Put the egg yolks and vanilla extract in a separate bowl and beat them together with a fork. Pour in the milk and combine well to incorporate everything.
7. In a smaller bowl mix the egg whites and cream of tartar with a fork. Fold into the egg yolks-milk mixture before adding in the flour mixture. Transfer equal amounts to the 6 soufflé dishes.
8. Put the dishes in the grill. Close the hood and BAKE for 15 minutes.
9. Serve warm.

Maple Walnut Pancake

Servings: 4

Cooking Time: 20 Minutes

Ingredients:

- 3 tablespoons melted butter, divided
- 1 cup flour
- 2 tablespoons sugar
- 1½ teaspoons baking powder
- ¼ teaspoon salt
- 1 egg, beaten
- ¾ cup milk
- 1 teaspoon pure vanilla extract
- ½ cup roughly chopped walnuts
- Maple syrup or fresh sliced fruit, for serving

Directions:

1. Select BAKE, set the temperature to 330°F, and set the time to 20 minutes. Select START/STOP to begin preheating.
2. Grease a baking pan with 1 tablespoon of melted butter.
3. Mix together the flour, sugar, baking powder, and salt in a medium bowl. Add the beaten egg, milk, the remaining 2 tablespoons of melted butter, and vanilla and stir until the batter is sticky but slightly lumpy.
4. Slowly pour the batter into the greased baking pan and scatter with the walnuts.
5. Place the pan directly in the pot. Close the hood and BAKE for 20 minutes until golden brown and cooked through.
6. Let the pancake rest for 5 minutes and serve topped with the maple syrup or fresh fruit, if desired.

English Pumpkin Egg Bake

Servings: 2

Cooking Time: 10 Minutes

Ingredients:

- 2 eggs
- ½ cup milk
- 2 cups flour
- 2 tablespoons cider vinegar
- 2 teaspoons baking powder
- 1 tablespoon sugar
- 1 cup pumpkin purée
- 1 teaspoon cinnamon powder
- 1 teaspoon baking soda
- 1 tablespoon olive oil

Directions:

1. Select BAKE, set the temperature to 300ºF, and set the time to 10 minutes. Select START/STOP to begin preheating.
2. Crack the eggs into a bowl and beat with a whisk. Combine with the milk, flour, cider vinegar, baking powder, sugar, pumpkin purée, cinnamon powder, and baking soda, mixing well.
3. Grease a baking pan with oil. Add the mixture to the pan. Place the pan directly in the pot. Close the hood and BAKE for 10 minutes.
4. Serve warm.

Honey-lime Glazed Grilled Fruit Salad

Servings: 4

Cooking Time: 4 Minutes

Ingredients:

- ½ pound strawberries, washed, hulled and halved
- 1 can pineapple chunks, drained, juice reserved
- 2 peaches, pitted and sliced
- 6 tablespoons honey, divided
- 1 tablespoon freshly squeezed lime juice

Directions:

1. Insert the Grill Grate and close the hood. Select GRILL, set the temperature to MAX, and set the time to 4 minutes. Select START/STOP to begin preheating.
2. While the unit is preheating, combine the strawberries, pineapple, and peaches in a large bowl with 3 tablespoons of honey. Toss to coat evenly.
3. When the unit beeps to signify it has preheated, place the fruit on the Grill Grate. Gently press the fruit down to maximize grill marks. Close the hood and GRILL for 4 minutes without flipping.
4. Meanwhile, in a small bowl, combine the remaining 3 tablespoons of honey, lime juice, and 1 tablespoon of reserved pineapple juice.
5. When cooking is complete, place the fruit in a large bowl and toss with the honey mixture. Serve immediately.

Fluffy Pancake Sheet

Servings: 4

Cooking Time: 12 Minutes

Ingredients:

- 3 cups pancake mix
- 1½ cups milk
- 2 eggs
- Nonstick cooking spray
- Unsalted butter, for topping
- Maple syrup, for topping

Directions:

1. Insert the Cooking Pot and close the hood. Select BAKE, set the temperature to 350°F, and set the time to 12 minutes. Select START/STOP to begin preheating.
2. While the unit is preheating, in a large bowl, whisk together the pancake mix, milk, and eggs.
3. When the unit beeps to signify it has preheated, spray the Cooking Pot with cooking spray. Pour the batter into the pot. Close the hood and cook for 12 minutes.
4. When cooking is complete, cut the pancake into squares. Top with the butter and maple syrup and serve.

Sides, Snacks & Appetizers

Sides, Snacks & Appetizers

Garlic Fries

Servings: 4

Cooking Time: 20 Minutes

Ingredients:

- 2 large Idaho or russet potatoes (1½ to 2 pounds)
- 1 head garlic (10 to 12 cloves)
- 4 tablespoons avocado oil, divided
- 1 teaspoon sea salt
- Chopped fresh parsley, for garnish

Directions:

1. Cut the potatoes into ¼-inch-thick slices. Place the slices in a large bowl and cover with cold water. Set aside for 30 minutes. This will ensure the potatoes cook well and crisp up perfectly. While the potatoes are soaking, mince the garlic cloves.
2. Drain the potatoes and pat dry using paper towels. In a large bowl, toss the potato slices with 2 tablespoons of avocado oil.
3. Insert the Cooking Pot and Crisper Basket and close the hood. Select AIR CRISP, set the temperature to 390°F, and set the time to 20 minutes. Select START/STOP to begin preheating.
4. While the unit is preheating, in a small bowl, combine the remaining 2 tablespoons of avocado oil with the minced garlic.
5. When the unit beeps to signify it has preheated, put the fries in the Crisper Basket. Close the hood and cook for 10 minutes.
6. After 10 minutes, open the hood and give the basket a shake to toss the fries. Close the hood and continue cooking for 5 minutes. Open the hood again and give the basket a shake. Close the hood and cook for 5 minutes more.
7. When cooking is complete, the fries will be crispy and golden brown. If you like them extra-crispy, continue cooking to your liking. Transfer the fries to a large bowl and drizzle with the garlic oil. Toss and season with the salt. Garnish with the parsley and serve.

Cheesy Summer Squash With Red Onion

Servings: 4

Cooking Time: 15 Minutes

Ingredients:

- ½ cup vegetable oil, plus 3 tablespoons
- ¼ cup white wine vinegar
- 1 garlic clove, grated
- 2 summer squash, sliced lengthwise about ¼-inch thick
- 1 red onion, peeled and cut into wedges
- Sea salt, to taste
- Freshly ground black pepper, to taste
- 1 package crumbled feta cheese
- Red pepper flakes, as needed

Directions:

1. Insert the Grill Grate and close the hood. Select GRILL, set the temperature to MAX, and set the time to 15 minutes. Select START/STOP to begin preheating.
2. Meanwhile, in a small bowl, whisk together ½ cup oil, vinegar, and garlic, and set aside.
3. In a large bowl, toss the squash and onion with remaining 3 tablespoons of oil until evenly coated. Season with the salt and pepper.
4. When the unit beeps to signify it has preheated, arrange the squash and onions on the Grill Grate. Close the hood and GRILL for 6 minutes.
5. After 6 minutes, open the hood and flip the squash. Close the hood and GRILL for 6 to 9 minutes more.
6. When vegetables are cooked to desired doneness, remove them from the grill. Arrange the vegetables on a large platter and top with the feta cheese. Drizzle the dressing over the top, and sprinkle with the red pepper flakes. Let stand for 15 minutes before serving.

Grilled Carrots With Honey Glazed

Servings: 4

Cooking Time: 10 Minutes

Ingredients:

- 6 medium carrots, peeled and cut lengthwise
- 1 tablespoon canola oil
- 2 tablespoons unsalted butter, melted
- ¼ cup brown sugar, melted
- ¼ cup honey
- ⅛ teaspoon sea salt

Directions:

1. Insert the Grill Grate and close the hood. Select GRILL, set the temperature to MAX, and set the time to 10 minutes. Select START/STOP to begin preheating.
2. In a large bowl, toss the carrots and oil until well coated.
3. When the unit beeps to signify it has preheated, place carrots on the center of the Grill Grate. Close the hood and GRILL for 5 minutes.
4. Meanwhile, in a small bowl, whisk together the butter, brown sugar, honey, and salt.
5. After 5 minutes, open the hood and baste the carrots with the glaze. Using tongs, turn the carrots and baste the other side. Close the hood and GRILL for another 5 minutes.
6. When cooking is complete, serve immediately.

Breaded Green Olives

Servings: 4

Cooking Time: 8 Minutes

Ingredients:

- 1 jar pitted green olives
- ½ cup all-purpose flour
- Salt and pepper, to taste
- ½ cup bread crumbs
- 1 egg
- Cooking spray

Directions:

1. Insert the Crisper Basket and close the hood. Select AIR CRISP, set the temperature to 400°F, and set the time to 8 minutes. Select START/STOP to begin preheating.
2. Remove the olives from the jar and dry thoroughly with paper towels.
3. In a small bowl, combine the flour with salt and pepper to taste. Place the bread crumbs in another small bowl. In a third small bowl, beat the egg.
4. Spritz the Crisper Basket with cooking spray.
5. Dip the olives in the flour, then the egg, and then the bread crumbs.
6. Place the breaded olives in the basket. It is okay to stack them. Spray the olives with cooking spray. Close the hood and AIR CRISP for 6 minutes. Flip the olives and AIR CRISP for an additional 2 minutes, or until brown and crisp.
7. Cool before serving.

Zucchini And Potato Tots

Servings: 4

Cooking Time: 20 Minutes

Ingredients:

- 1 large zucchini, grated
- 1 medium baked potato, skin removed and mashed
- ¼ cup shredded Cheddar cheese
- 1 large egg, beaten
- ½ teaspoon kosher salt
- Cooking spray

Directions:

1. Select AIR CRISP, set the temperature to 390°F, and set the time to 10 minutes. Select START/STOP to begin preheating.
2. Wrap the grated zucchini in a paper towel and squeeze out any excess liquid, then combine the zucchini, baked potato, shredded Cheddar cheese, egg, and kosher salt in a large bowl.
3. Spray a baking pan with cooking spray, then place individual tablespoons of the zucchini mixture in the pan. Place the pan directly in the pot. Close the hood and AIR CRISP for 10 minutes. Repeat this process with the remaining mixture.
4. Remove the tots and allow to cool on a wire rack for 5 minutes before serving.

Cajun Zucchini Chips

Servings: 4

Cooking Time: 15 To 16 Minutes

Ingredients:

- 2 large zucchini, cut into ⅛-inch-thick slices
- 2 teaspoons Cajun seasoning
- Cooking spray

Directions:

1. Spray the Crisper Basket lightly with cooking spray.
2. Insert the Crisper Basket and close the hood. Select AIR CRISP, set the temperature to 370°F, and set the time to 16 minutes. Select START/STOP to begin preheating.
3. Put the zucchini slices in a medium bowl and spray them generously with cooking spray.
4. Sprinkle the Cajun seasoning over the zucchini and stir to make sure they are evenly coated with oil and seasoning.
5. Place the slices in a single layer in the Crisper Basket, making sure not to overcrowd. You will need to cook these in several batches.
6. Close the hood and AIR CRISP for 8 minutes. Flip the slices over and AIR CRISP for an additional 7 to 8 minutes, or until they are as crisp and brown as you prefer.
7. Serve immediately.

Cheesy Garlic Bread

Servings: 4

Cooking Time: 8 Minutes

Ingredients:

- 1 loaf (about 1 pound) French bread
- 8 tablespoons (1 stick) unsalted butter, at room temperature
- 1 tablespoon minced garlic
- 1 teaspoon garlic powder
- 1½ cups shredded mozzarella cheese
- ½ cup shredded Colby Jack cheese
- 1 teaspoon dried parsley

Directions:

1. Insert the Grill Grate and close the hood. Select GRILL, set the temperature to MED, and set the time to 8 minutes. Select START/STOP to begin preheating.
2. While the unit is preheating, cut the French bread in half lengthwise. In a small bowl, mix together the butter, garlic, and garlic powder until well combined. Spread the garlic butter on both bread halves. Top each half with the mozzarella and Colby Jack cheeses. Sprinkle the dried parsley on top.
3. When the unit beeps to signify it has preheated, place the cheese-topped bread on the Grill Grate. Close the hood and grill for 8 minutes.
4. When cooking is complete, the cheese will be melted and golden brown. Remove the bread from the grill and serve.

Cheesy Apple Roll-ups

Servings: 8

Cooking Time: 4 To 5 Minutes

Ingredients:

- 8 slices whole wheat sandwich bread
- 4 ounces Colby Jack cheese, grated
- ½ small apple, chopped
- 2 tablespoons butter, melted

Directions:

1. Insert the Crisper Basket and close the hood. Select AIR CRISP, set the temperature to 390°F, and set the time to 5 minutes. Select START/STOP to begin preheating.
2. Remove the crusts from the bread and flatten the slices with a rolling pin. Don't be gentle. Press hard so that bread will be very thin.
3. Top bread slices with cheese and chopped apple, dividing the ingredients evenly.
4. Roll up each slice tightly and secure each with one or two toothpicks.
5. Brush outside of rolls with melted butter.
6. Place in the Crisper Basket. Close the hood and AIR CRISP for 4 to 5 minutes, or until outside is crisp and nicely browned.
7. Serve hot.

Deluxe Cheese Sandwiches

Servings: 4 To 8

Cooking Time: 5 To 6 Minutes

Ingredients:

- 8 ounces Brie
- 8 slices oat nut bread
- 1 large ripe pear, cored and cut into ½-inch-thick slices
- 2 tablespoons butter, melted

Directions:

1. Select BAKE, set the temperature to 360°F, and set the time to 6 minutes. Select START/STOP to begin preheating. .
2. Make the sandwiches: Spread each of 4 slices of bread with ¼ of the Brie. Top the Brie with the pear slices and remaining 4 bread slices.
3. Brush the melted butter lightly on both sides of each sandwich.
4. Arrange the sandwiches in a baking pan. You may need to work in batches to avoid overcrowding.
5. Place the pan directly in the pot. Close the hood and BAKE for 5 to 6 minutes until the cheese is melted. Repeat with the remaining sandwiches.
6. Serve warm.

Sweet Potato Chips

Servings:1

Cooking Time: 8 To 10 Hours

Ingredients:

- 1 sweet potato, peeled
- ½ tablespoon avocado oil
- ½ teaspoon sea salt

Directions:

1. Using a mandoline, thinly slice (⅛ inch or less) the sweet potato.
2. In a large bowl, toss the sweet potato slices with the oil until evenly coated. Season with the salt.
3. Place the sweet potato slices flat on the Crisper Basket. Arrange them in a single layer, without any slices touching each another.
4. Place the basket in the pot and close the hood.
5. Select DEHYDRATE, set the temperature to 120°F, and set the time to 10 hours. Select START/STOP.
6. After 8 hours, check for desired doneness. Continue dehydrating for 2 more hours, if necessary.
7. When cooking is complete, remove the basket from the pot. Transfer the sweet potato chips to an airtight container and store at room temperature.

Cheesy Crab Toasts

Servings:15

Cooking Time: 5 Minutes

Ingredients:

- 1 can flaked crab meat, well drained
- 3 tablespoons light mayonnaise
- ¼ cup shredded Parmesan cheese
- ¼ cup shredded Cheddar cheese
- 1 teaspoon Worcestershire sauce
- ½ teaspoon lemon juice
- 1 loaf artisan bread, French bread, or baguette, cut into ⅜-inch-thick slices

Directions:

1. Insert the Crisper Basket and close the hood. Select BAKE, set the temperature to 360°F, and set the time to 5 minutes. Select START/STOP to begin preheating.
2. In a large bowl, stir together all the ingredients except the bread slices.
3. On a clean work surface, lay the bread slices. Spread ½ tablespoon of crab mixture onto each slice of bread.
4. Arrange the bread slices in the Crisper Basket in a single layer. You'll need to work in batches to avoid overcrowding.
5. Close the hood and BAKE for 5 minutes until the tops are lightly browned.
6. Transfer to a plate and repeat with the remaining bread slices.
7. Serve warm.

BBQ Grill & Smoker Cookbook

Cheesy Steak Fries

Servings: 5

Cooking Time: 20 Minutes

Ingredients:

- 1 bag frozen steak fries
- Cooking spray
- Salt and pepper, to taste
- ½ cup beef gravy
- 1 cup shredded Mozzarella cheese
- 2 scallions, green parts only, chopped

Directions:

1. Insert the Crisper Basket and close the hood. Select AIR CRISP, set the temperature to 400°F, and set the time to 20 minutes. Select START/STOP to begin preheating.
2. Place the frozen steak fries in the basket. Close the hood and AIR CRISP for 10 minutes. Shake the basket and spritz the fries with cooking spray. Sprinkle with salt and pepper. AIR CRISP for an additional 8 minutes.
3. Pour the beef gravy into a medium, microwave-safe bowl. Microwave for 30 seconds, or until the gravy is warm.
4. Sprinkle the fries with the cheese. Close the hood and AIR CRISP for an additional 2 minutes, until the cheese is melted.
5. Transfer the fries to a serving dish. Drizzle the fries with gravy and sprinkle the scallions on top for a green garnish. Serve.

French Fries

Servings: 4

Cooking Time: 25 Minutes

Ingredients:

- 1 pound russet or Idaho potatoes, cut in 2-inch strips
- 3 tablespoons canola oil

Directions:

1. Place the potatoes in a large bowl and cover them with cold water. Let soak for 30 minutes. Drain well, then pat with a paper towel until very dry.
2. Insert the Crisper Basket and close the hood. Select AIR CRISP, set the temperature to 390°F, and set the time to 25 minutes. Select START/STOP to begin preheating.
3. Meanwhile, in a large bowl, toss the potatoes with the oil.
4. When the unit beeps to signify it has preheated, add the potatoes to the basket. Close the hood and AIR CRISP for 10 minutes.
5. After 10 minutes, shake the basket well. Place the basket back in the unit and close the hood to resume cooking.
6. After 10 minutes, check for desired crispness. Continue cooking up to 5 minutes more, if necessary.
7. When cooking is complete, serve immediately with your favorite dipping sauce.

Roasted Mixed Nuts

Servings: 6

Cooking Time: 20 Minutes

Ingredients:

- 2 cups mixed nuts (walnuts, pecans, and almonds)
- 2 tablespoons egg white
- 2 tablespoons sugar
- 1 teaspoon paprika
- 1 teaspoon ground cinnamon
- Cooking spray

Directions:

1. Spray the Crisper Basket with cooking spray.
2. Insert the Crisper Basket and close the hood. Select ROAST, set the temperature to 300°F, and set the time to 20 minutes. Select START/STOP to begin preheating.
3. Stir together the mixed nuts, egg white, sugar, paprika, and cinnamon in a small bowl until the nuts are fully coated.
4. Put the nuts in the Crisper Basket. Close the hood and ROAST for 20 minutes. Shake the basket halfway through the cooking time for even cooking.
5. Transfer the nuts to a bowl and serve warm.

Mushroom And Spinach Calzones

Servings: 4

Cooking Time: 26 To 27 Minutes

Ingredients:

- 2 tablespoons olive oil
- 1 onion, chopped
- 2 garlic cloves, minced
- ¼ cup chopped mushrooms
- 1 pound spinach, chopped
- 1 tablespoon Italian seasoning
- ½ teaspoon oregano
- Salt and black pepper, to taste
- 1½ cups marinara sauce
- 1 cup ricotta cheese, crumbled
- 1 pizza crust
- Cooking spray

Directions:

1. Make the Filling:
2. Heat the olive oil in a pan over medium heat until shimmering.
3. Add the onion, garlic, and mushrooms and sauté for 4 minutes, or until softened.
4. Stir in the spinach and sauté for 2 to 3 minutes, or until the spinach is wilted. Sprinkle with the Italian seasoning, oregano, salt, and pepper and mix well.
5. Add the marinara sauce and cook for about 5 minutes, stirring occasionally, or until the sauce is thickened.
6. Remove the pan from the heat and stir in the ricotta cheese. Set aside.
7. Make the Calzones:
8. Spritz the Crisper Basket with cooking spray.
9. Insert the Crisper Basket and close the hood. Select AIR CRISP, set the temperature to 375ºF, and set the time to 15 minutes. Select START/STOP to begin preheating.
10. Roll the pizza crust out with a rolling pin on a lightly floured work surface, then cut it into 4 rectangles.
11. Spoon ¼ of the filling into each rectangle and fold in half. Crimp the edges with a fork to seal. Mist them with cooking spray.
12. Place the calzones in the Crisper Basket. Close the hood and AIR CRISP for 15 minutes, flipping once, or until the calzones are golden brown and crisp.
13. Transfer the calzones to a paper towel-lined plate and serve.

Sausage And Mushroom Empanadas

Servings: 4

Cooking Time: 12 Minutes

Ingredients:

- ½ pound Kielbasa smoked sausage, chopped
- 4 chopped canned mushrooms
- 2 tablespoons chopped onion
- ½ teaspoon ground cumin
- ¼ teaspoon paprika
- Salt and black pepper, to taste
- ½ package puff pastry dough, at room temperature
- 1 egg, beaten
- Cooking spray

Directions:

1. Spritz the Crisper Basket with cooking spray.
2. Insert the Crisper Basket and close the hood. Select AIR CRISP, set the temperature to 360ºF, and set the time to 12 minutes. Select START/STOP to begin preheating.
3. Combine the sausage, mushrooms, onion, cumin, paprika, salt, and pepper in a bowl and stir to mix well.
4. Make the empanadas: Place the puff pastry dough on a lightly floured surface. Cut circles into the dough with a glass. Place 1 tablespoon of the sausage mixture into the center of each pastry circle. Fold each in half and pinch the edges to seal. Using a fork, crimp the edges. Brush them with the beaten egg and mist with cooking spray.
5. Place the empanadas in the Crisper Basket. Close the hood and AIR CRISP for 12 minutes until golden brown. Flip the empanadas halfway through the cooking time.
6. Allow them to cool for 5 minutes and serve hot.

Cuban Sandwiches

Servings: 4

Cooking Time: 8 Minutes

Ingredients:

- 8 slices ciabatta bread, about ¼-inch thick
- Cooking spray
- 1 tablespoon brown mustard
- Toppings:
- 6 to 8 ounces thinly sliced leftover roast pork
- 4 ounces thinly sliced deli turkey
- ⅓ cup bread and butter pickle slices
- 2 to 3 ounces Pepper Jack cheese slices

Directions:

1. Insert the Crisper Basket and close the hood. Select AIR CRISP, set the temperature to 390°F, and set the time to 8 minutes. Select START/STOP to begin preheating.
2. On a clean work surface, spray one side of each slice of bread with cooking spray. Spread the other side of each slice of bread evenly with brown mustard.
3. Top 4 of the bread slices with the roast pork, turkey, pickle slices, cheese, and finish with remaining bread slices. Transfer to the Crisper Basket.
4. Close the hood and AIR CRISP for 8 minutes until golden brown.
5. Cool for 5 minutes and serve warm.

Grilled Shishito Peppers

Servings: 4

Cooking Time: 10 Minutes

Ingredients:

- 3 cups whole shishito peppers
- 2 tablespoons vegetable oil
- Flaky sea salt, for garnish

Directions:

1. Insert the Grill Grate and close the hood. Select GRILL, set the temperature to MAX, and set the time to 10 minutes. Select START/STOP to begin preheating.
2. While the unit is preheating, in a medium bowl, toss the peppers in the oil until evenly coated.
3. When the unit beeps to signify it has preheated, place the peppers on the Grill Grate. Gently press the peppers down to maximize grill marks. Close the hood and GRILL for 8 to 10 minutes, until they are blistered on all sides.
4. When cooking is complete, place the peppers in a serving dish and top with the flaky sea salt. Serve immediately.

Queso Bomb

Servings: 6

Cooking Time: 15 Minutes

Ingredients:

- 1 (1-pound) block easy-melt cheese
- 1 pound ground country breakfast sausage (not links)
- 2 tablespoons minced garlic
- 2 cups shredded Mexican cheese blend or three-cheese blend
- 1 (10-ounce) can diced tomatoes with green chiles
- 1 (10- to 13-ounce) bag tortilla chips

Directions:

1. Insert the Cooking Pot and close the hood. Select GRILL, set the temperature to MED, and set the time to 15 minutes. Select START/STOP to begin preheating.
2. While the unit is preheating, slice the cheese block into 3-inch sections.
3. When the unit beeps to signify it has preheated, place the sausage and garlic in the Cooking Pot. Using a wooden spoon or spatula, break the sausage apart. Close the hood and cook for 5 minutes.
4. After 5 minutes, open the hood and stir the sausage. Add the pieces of easy-melt cheese, then add the shredded cheese blend in an even layer. Pour the diced tomatoes and green chiles with their juices into the pot. Close the hood and cook for 5 minutes.
5. After 5 minutes, stir the sausage and cheese together. Close the hood and cook 5 minutes more.
6. When cooking is complete, the cheese will be fully melted. Serve warm with tortilla chips.

Mozzarella Sticks

Servings: 4

Cooking Time: 8 Minutes

Ingredients:

- 2 large eggs
- 2 cups plain bread crumbs
- 2 tablespoons Italian seasoning
- 10 to 12 mozzarella cheese sticks
- Marinara sauce, for dipping

Directions:

1. In a large bowl, whisk the eggs. In a separate large bowl, combine the bread crumbs and Italian seasoning.
2. Dip each cheese stick in the egg and then dip it in the bread crumbs to evenly coat. Place the breaded mozzarella sticks on a baking sheet or flat tray, then freeze for 30 minutes.
3. Insert the Grill Grate and close the hood. Select GRILL, set the temperature to MED, and set the time to 8 minutes. Select START/STOP to begin preheating.
4. When the unit beeps to signify it has preheated, open the hood and place the mozzarella sticks on the Grill Grate. Close the hood and grill for 8 minutes.
5. When cooking is complete, the mozzarella sticks will be golden brown and crispy. If you prefer browner mozzarella sticks, continue cooking to your liking. Serve with the marinara sauce on the side.

Spicy Kale Chips

Servings: 4

Cooking Time: 8 To 12 Minutes

Ingredients:

- 5 cups kale, large stems removed and chopped
- 2 teaspoons canola oil
- ¼ teaspoon smoked paprika
- ¼ teaspoon kosher salt
- Cooking spray

Directions:

1. Insert the Crisper Basket and close the hood. Select AIR CRISP, set the temperature to 390°F, and set the time to 6 minutes. Select START/STOP to begin preheating.
2. In a large bowl, toss the kale, canola oil, smoked paprika, and kosher salt.
3. Spray the Crisper Basket with cooking spray, then place half the kale in the basket. Close the hood and AIR CRISP for 2 to 3 minutes.
4. Shake the basket and AIR CRISP for 2 to 3 more minutes, or until crispy. Repeat this process with the remaining kale.
5. Remove the kale and allow to cool on a wire rack for 3 to 5 minutes before serving.

Blistered Lemony Green Beans

Servings: 4

Cooking Time: 10 Minutes

Ingredients:

- 1 pound haricots verts or green beans, trimmed
- 2 tablespoons vegetable oil
- Juice of 1 lemon
- Pinch red pepper flakes
- Flaky sea salt, to taste
- Freshly ground black pepper, to taste

Directions:

1. Insert the Grill Grate and close the hood. Select GRILL, set the temperature to MAX, and set the time to 10 minutes. Select START/STOP to begin preheating.
2. While the unit is preheating, in a medium bowl, toss the green beans in oil until evenly coated.
3. When the unit beeps to signify it has preheated, place the green beans on the Grill Grate. Close the hood and GRILL for 8 to 10 minutes, tossing frequently until blistered on all sides.
4. When cooking is complete, place the green beans on a large serving platter. Squeeze lemon juice over the green beans, top with red pepper flakes, and season with sea salt and black pepper.

Dill Pickles

Servings: 4

Cooking Time: 10 Minutes

Ingredients:

- 20 dill pickle slices
- ¼ cup all-purpose flour
- ⅛ teaspoon baking powder
- 3 tablespoons beer or seltzer water
- ⅛ teaspoon sea salt
- 2 tablespoons water, plus more if needed
- 2 tablespoons cornstarch
- 1½ cups panko bread crumbs
- 1 teaspoon paprika
- 1 teaspoon garlic powder
- ¼ teaspoon cayenne pepper
- 2 tablespoons canola oil, divided

Directions:

1. Pat the pickle slices dry, and place them on a dry plate in the freezer.
2. In a medium bowl, stir together the flour, baking powder, beer, salt, and water. The batter should be the consistency of cake batter. If it is too thick, add more water, 1 teaspoon at a time.
3. Place the cornstarch in a small shallow bowl.
4. In a separate large shallow bowl, combine the bread crumbs, paprika, garlic powder, and cayenne pepper.
5. Remove the pickles from the freezer. Dredge each one in cornstarch. Tap off any excess, then coat in the batter. Lastly, coat evenly with the bread crumb mixture.
6. Insert the Crisper Basket and close the hood. Select AIR CRISP, set the temperature to 360°F, and set the time to 10 minutes. Select START/STOP to begin preheating.
7. When the unit beeps to signify it has preheated, place the breaded pickles in the basket, stacking them if necessary, and gently brush them with 1 tablespoon of oil. Close the hood and AIR CRISP for 5 minutes.
8. After 5 minutes, shake the basket and gently brush the pickles with the remaining 1 tablespoon of oil. Place the basket back in the unit and close the hood to resume cooking.
9. When cooking is complete, serve immediately.

Creamy Artichoke Dip With Pita Chips

Servings: 4

Cooking Time: 15 Minutes

Ingredients:

- 8 ounces cream cheese, at room temperature
- 1 (13-ounce) can marinated artichoke quarters, drained and coarsely chopped
- ½ cup sour cream
- ½ cup grated Parmesan cheese
- ¼ teaspoon garlic powder
- 2 cups shredded mozzarella
- 1 (6-ounce) package mini pita bread rounds
- Extra-virgin olive oil
- Chopped fresh chives, for garnish

Directions:

1. Insert the Cooking Pot and close the hood. Select GRILL, set the temperature to MED, and set the time to 15 minutes. Select START/STOP to begin preheating.
2. While the unit is preheating, place the cream cheese, artichokes, sour cream, Parmesan cheese, garlic powder, and mozzarella cheese in a 9-by-5-inch loaf pan. Stir until well combined.
3. When the unit beeps to signify it has preheated, place the pan in the Cooking Pot. Close the hood and cook for 5 minutes.
4. After 5 minutes, open the hood and stir the dip with a wooden spoon, holding onto the loaf pan with grill mitts. Close the hood and cook for 7 minutes more.
5. Meanwhile, place the Grill Grate next to the Foodi™ Grill. Put the pita rounds in a large bowl and drizzle with the olive oil. Toss to coat. Place the pita rounds on the Grill Grate.
6. After 7 minutes, open the hood. Remove the pan of artichoke dip from the Cooking Pot. Place the Grill Grate into the unit. Close the hood and cook for the remaining 3 minutes.
7. Cooking is complete when the pita chips are warm and crispy. Garnish the dip with the fresh chives and serve.

Homemade Bbq Chicken Pizza

Servings: 1

Cooking Time: 8 Minutes

Ingredients:

- 1 piece naan bread
- ¼ cup Barbecue sauce
- ¼ cup shredded Monterrey Jack cheese
- ¼ cup shredded Mozzarella cheese
- ½ chicken herby sausage, sliced
- 2 tablespoons red onion, thinly sliced
- Chopped cilantro or parsley, for garnish
- Cooking spray

Directions:

1. Insert the Crisper Basket and close the hood. Select AIR CRISP, set the temperature to 400ºF, and set the time to 8 minutes. Select START/STOP to begin preheating.
2. Spritz the bottom of naan bread with cooking spray, then transfer to the Crisper Basket.
3. Brush with the Barbecue sauce. Top with the cheeses, sausage, and finish with the red onion.
4. Close the hood and AIR CRISP for 8 minutes until the cheese is melted.
5. Garnish with the chopped cilantro or parsley before slicing to serve.

Crispy Cod Fingers

Servings: 4

Cooking Time: 12 Minutes

Ingredients:

- 2 eggs
- 2 tablespoons milk
- 2 cups flour
- 1 cup cornmeal
- 1 teaspoon seafood seasoning
- Salt and black pepper, to taste
- 1 cup bread crumbs
- 1 pound cod fillets, cut into 1-inch strips

Directions:

1. Insert the Crisper Basket and close the hood. Select AIR CRISP, set the temperature to 400ºF, and set the time to 12 minutes. Select START/STOP to begin preheating.
2. Beat the eggs with the milk in a shallow bowl. In another shallow bowl, combine the flour, cornmeal, seafood seasoning, salt, and pepper. On a plate, place the bread crumbs.
3. Dredge the cod strips, one at a time, in the flour mixture, then in the egg mixture, finally in the bread crumb to coat evenly.
4. Arrange the cod strips in the Crisper Basket. Close the hood and AIR CRISP for 12 minutes until crispy.
5. Transfer the cod strips to a paper towel-lined plate and serve warm.

Rosemary Baked Cashews

Servings: 2

Cooking Time: 3 Minutes

Ingredients:

- 2 sprigs of fresh rosemary
- 1 teaspoon olive oil
- 1 teaspoon kosher salt
- ½ teaspoon honey
- 2 cups roasted and unsalted whole cashews
- Cooking spray

Directions:

1. Insert the Crisper Basket and close the hood. Select BAKE, set the temperature to 300ºF, and set the time to 3 minutes. Select START/STOP to begin preheating.
2. In a medium bowl, whisk together the chopped rosemary, olive oil, kosher salt, and honey. Set aside.
3. Spray the Crisper Basket with cooking spray, then place the cashews and the whole rosemary sprig in the basket. Close the hood and BAKE for 3 minutes.
4. Remove the cashews and rosemary from the grill, then discard the rosemary and add the cashews to the olive oil mixture, tossing to coat.
5. Allow to cool for 15 minutes before serving.

Jalapeño Poppers

Servings: 4

Cooking Time: 10 Minutes

Ingredients:

- 8 jalapeños
- 4 ounces cream cheese, at room temperature
- ¼ cup grated Parmesan cheese
- ¼ cup shredded cheddar cheese
- ½ teaspoon garlic powder
- 8 slices thin-cut bacon

Directions:

1. Insert the Grill Grate and close the hood. Select GRILL, set the temperature to HI, and set the time to 10 minutes. Select START/STOP to begin preheating.
2. While the unit is preheating, slice the jalapeños in half lengthwise and scoop out the seeds and membranes.
3. In a small bowl, combine the cream cheese, Parmesan cheese, cheddar cheese, and garlic powder. Scoop the cheese mixture evenly into each jalapeño half.
4. Slice the bacon in half lengthwise so you have 16 strips. Wrap each jalapeño half with a bacon slice, starting from the bottom end and wrapping around until it reaches the top of the jalapeño.
5. When the unit beeps to signify it has preheated, place the jalapeños on the Grill Grate, filling-side up. Close the hood and grill for 10 minutes.
6. When cooking is complete, the bacon will be cooked and beginning to crisp. If you prefer your bacon crispier or charred, continue cooking to your liking. Remove the poppers from the grill and serve.

Bacon-wrapped Dates

Servings: 6

Cooking Time: 10 To 14 Minutes

Ingredients:

- 12 dates, pitted
- 6 slices high-quality bacon, cut in half
- Cooking spray

Directions:

1. Insert the Crisper Basket and close the hood. Select BAKE, set the temperature to 360°F, and set the time to 7 minutes. Select START/STOP to begin preheating.
2. Wrap each date with half a bacon slice and secure with a toothpick.
3. Spray the Crisper Basket with cooking spray, then place 6 bacon-wrapped dates in the basket. Place the pan directly in the pot. Close the hood and BAKE for 5 to 7 minutes or until the bacon is crispy. Repeat this process with the remaining dates.
4. Remove the dates and allow to cool on a wire rack for 5 minutes before serving.

Brussels Sprouts And Bacon

Servings: 4

Cooking Time: 12 Minutes

Ingredients:

- 1 pound Brussels sprouts, trimmed and halved
- 2 tablespoons extra-virgin olive oil
- 1 teaspoon sea salt
- ½ teaspoon freshly ground black pepper
- 6 slices bacon, chopped

Directions:

1. Insert the Crisper Basket and close the hood. Select AIR CRISP, set the temperature to 390°F, and set the time to 12 minutes. Select START/STOP to begin preheating.
2. Meanwhile, in a large bowl, toss the Brussels sprouts with the olive oil, salt, pepper, and bacon.
3. When the unit beeps to signify it has preheated, add the Brussels sprouts to the basket. Close the hood and AIR CRISP for 10 minutes.
4. After 6 minutes, shake the basket of Brussels sprouts. Place the basket back in the unit and close the hood to resume cooking.
5. After 6 minutes, check for desired crispness. Continue cooking up to 2 more minutes, if necessary.

Twice Air-crisped Potatoes

Servings: 4

Cooking Time: 40 Minutes

Ingredients:

- 4 medium Idaho or russet potatoes
- Extra-virgin olive oil
- Kosher salt
- 8 tablespoons (1 stick) unsalted butter, at room temperature
- ½ cup sour cream
- 1 cup shredded cheddar cheese
- Freshly ground black pepper

Directions:

1. Insert the Crisper Basket and close the hood. Select AIR CRISP, set the temperature to 400°F, and set the time to 40 minutes. Select START/STOP to begin preheating.
2. While the unit is preheating, rinse and scrub the potatoes. Poke each potato several times with a fork. Brush a generous amount of olive oil over the potatoes and season well with salt.
3. When the unit beeps to signify it has preheated, place the potatoes in the Crisper Basket. Close the hood and cook for 30 minutes.
4. After 30 minutes, open the hood and remove the potatoes. Place on a plate and set aside.
5. Slice the potatoes in half lengthwise. Use a fork to carefully scoop out the insides of the potatoes without damaging the skins. Put the potato flesh in a large bowl. Add the butter, sour cream, and cheddar cheese. Using a spatula, carefully fold the mixture until the butter melts. Scoop the filling into the potato skins. Season each potato half with salt and pepper.
6. Place the loaded potatoes back into the Crisper Basket. Close the hood and cook for 10 minutes more.
7. When cooking is complete, the potato skins will be crispy and the cheese will be melted and infused into the potatoes. Remove the potatoes from the grill and serve.

Bacon-wrapped Onion Rings And Spicy Aioli

Servings: 4

Cooking Time: 10 Minutes

Ingredients:

- For the onion rings
- 3 large white onions
- 2 (1-pound) packages thin-sliced bacon
- For the spicy garlic aioli sauce
- 1 cup mayonnaise
- ¼ teaspoon garlic powder
- 1 tablespoon sriracha
- 1 teaspoon freshly squeezed lemon juice

Directions:

1. Insert the Grill Grate and close the hood. Select GRILL, set the temperature to MED, and set the time to 10 minutes. Select START/STOP to begin preheating.
2. While the unit is preheating, cut both ends off the onions. Slice each onion crosswise into thirds and peel off the outer layer of onion skin. Separate the onion rings, keeping two onion layers together to have a stable and firm ring. Wrap each onion ring pair with a slice of bacon. The bacon should slightly overlap itself as you wrap it all the way around the onion ring. Larger rings may need 2 slices of bacon.
3. When the unit beeps to signify it has preheated, place the onion rings on the Grill Grate. Close the hood and grill for 10 minutes. Flipping is not necessary.
4. When cooking is complete, the bacon will be cooked through and starting to crisp. If you prefer the bacon crispier or even close to charred, continue cooking to your liking.
5. While the onion rings are cooking, in a small bowl, whisk together the mayonnaise, garlic powder, sriracha, and lemon juice. Use more or less sriracha depending on your preferred spice level. Serve with the bacon onion rings.

BBQ Grill & Smoker Cookbook

Meatless

Meatless

Cheesy Asparagus And Potato Platter

Servings: 5

Cooking Time: 26 To 30 Minutes

Ingredients:

- 4 medium potatoes, cut into wedges
- Cooking spray
- 1 bunch asparagus, trimmed
- 2 tablespoons olive oil
- Salt and pepper, to taste
- Cheese Sauce:
- ¼ cup crumbled cottage cheese
- ¼ cup buttermilk
- 1 tablespoon whole-grain mustard
- Salt and black pepper, to taste

Directions:

1. Insert the Crisper Basket and close the hood. Select ROAST, set the temperature to 400ºF, and set the time to 30 minutes. Select START/STOP to begin preheating.
2. Spritz the Crisper Basket with cooking spray.
3. Put the potatoes in the Crisper Basket. Close the hood and ROAST for 20 to 22 minutes, until golden brown. Shake the basket halfway through the cooking time.
4. When ready, remove the potatoes from the basket to a platter. Cover the potatoes with foil to keep warm. Set aside.
5. Place the asparagus in the Crisper Basket and drizzle with the olive oil. Sprinkle with salt and pepper.
6. Close the hood and ROAST for 6 to 8 minutes, shaking the basket once or twice during cooking, or until the asparagus is cooked to your desired crispiness.
7. Meanwhile, make the cheese sauce by stirring together the cottage cheese, buttermilk, and mustard in a small bowl. Season with salt and pepper.
8. Transfer the asparagus to the platter of potatoes and drizzle with the cheese sauce. Serve immediately.

Stuffed Squash With Tomatoes And Poblano

Servings: 4

Cooking Time: 30 Minutes

Ingredients:

- 1 pound butternut squash, ends trimmed
- 2 teaspoons olive oil, divided
- 6 grape tomatoes, halved
- 1 poblano pepper, cut into strips
- Salt and black pepper, to taste
- ¼ cup grated Mozzarella cheese

Directions:

1. Insert the Crisper Basket and close the hood. Select ROAST, set the temperature to 350ºF, and set the time to 30 minutes. Select START/STOP to begin preheating.
2. Using a large knife, cut the squash in half lengthwise on a flat work surface. This recipe just needs half of the squash. Scoop out the flesh to make room for the stuffing. Coat the squash half with 1 teaspoon of olive oil.
3. Put the squash half in the Crisper Basket. Close the hood and ROAST for 15 minutes.
4. Meanwhile, thoroughly combine the tomatoes, poblano pepper, remaining 1 teaspoon of olive oil, salt, and pepper in a bowl.
5. Remove the basket and spoon the tomato mixture into the squash. Return to the grill and roast for 12 minutes until the tomatoes are soft.
6. Scatter the Mozzarella cheese on top and continue roasting for about 3 minutes, or until the cheese is melted.
7. Cool for 5 minutes before serving.

Summer Squash And Zucchini Salad

Servings: 4

Cooking Time: 20 Minutes

Ingredients:

- 1 zucchini, sliced lengthwise about ¼-inch thick
- 1 summer squash, sliced lengthwise about ¼-inch thick
- ½ red onion, sliced
- 4 tablespoons canola oil, divided
- 2 portobello mushroom caps, trimmed with gills removed
- 2 ears corn, shucked
- 2 teaspoons freshly squeezed lemon juice
- Sea salt, to taste
- Freshly ground black pepper, to taste

Directions:

1. Insert the Grill Grate and close the hood. Select GRILL, set the temperature to MAX, and set the time to 25 minutes. Select START/STOP to begin preheating.
2. Meanwhile, in a large bowl, toss the zucchini, squash, and onion with 2 tablespoons of oil until evenly coated.
3. When the unit beeps to signify it has preheated, arrange the zucchini, squash, and onions on the Grill Grate. Close the hood and GRILL for 6 minutes.
4. After 6 minutes, open the hood and flip the squash. Close the hood and GRILL for 6 to 9 minutes more.
5. Meanwhile, brush the mushrooms and corn with the remaining 2 tablespoons of oil.
6. When cooking is complete, remove the zucchini, squash, and onions and swap in the mushrooms and corn. Close the hood and GRILL for the remaining 10 minutes.
7. When cooking is complete, remove the mushrooms and corn, and let cool.
8. Cut the kernels from the cobs. Roughly chop all the vegetables into bite-size pieces.
9. Place the vegetables in a serving bowl and drizzle with lemon juice. Season with salt and pepper, and toss until evenly mixed.

Honey-glazed Roasted Veggies

Servings: 3

Cooking Time: 20 Minutes

Ingredients:

- Glaze:
- 2 tablespoons raw honey
- 2 teaspoons minced garlic
- ¼ teaspoon dried marjoram
- ¼ teaspoon dried basil
- ¼ teaspoon dried oregano
- ⅛ teaspoon dried sage
- ⅛ teaspoon dried rosemary
- ⅛ teaspoon dried thyme
- ½ teaspoon salt
- ¼ teaspoon ground black pepper
- Veggies:
- 3 to 4 medium red potatoes, cut into 1- to 2-inch pieces
- 1 small zucchini, cut into 1- to 2-inch pieces
- 1 small carrot, sliced into ¼-inch rounds
- 1 package cherry tomatoes, halved
- 1 cup sliced mushrooms
- 3 tablespoons olive oil

Directions:

1. Insert the Crisper Basket and close the hood. Select ROAST, set the temperature to 380ºF, and set the time to 15 minutes. Select START/STOP to begin preheating.
2. Combine the honey, garlic, marjoram, basil, oregano, sage, rosemary, thyme, salt, and pepper in a small bowl and stir to mix well. Set aside.
3. Place the red potatoes, zucchini, carrot, cherry tomatoes, and mushroom in a large bowl. Drizzle with the olive oil and toss to coat.
4. Pour the veggies into the Crisper Basket. Close the hood and ROAST for 15 minutes, shaking the basket halfway through.
5. When ready, transfer the roasted veggies to the large bowl. Pour the honey mixture over the veggies, tossing to coat.
6. Spread out the veggies in a baking pan and place in the grill.
7. Increase the temperature to 390ºF and ROAST for an additional 5 minutes, or until the veggies are tender and glazed. Serve warm.

Asian-inspired Broccoli

Servings: 2

Cooking Time: 10 Minutes

Ingredients:

- 12 ounces broccoli florets
- 2 tablespoons Asian hot chili oil
- 1 teaspoon ground Sichuan peppercorns (or black pepper)
- 2 garlic cloves, finely chopped
- 1 piece fresh ginger, peeled and finely chopped
- Kosher salt and freshly ground black pepper

Directions:

1. Insert the Crisper Basket and close the hood. Select ROAST, set the temperature to 375°F, and set the time to 10 minutes. Select START/STOP to begin preheating.
2. Toss the broccoli florets with the chili oil, Sichuan peppercorns, garlic, ginger, salt, and pepper in a mixing bowl until thoroughly coated.
3. Transfer the broccoli florets to the Crisper Basket. Close the hood and ROAST for 10 minutes, shaking the basket halfway through, or until the broccoli florets are lightly browned and tender.
4. Remove the broccoli from the basket and serve on a plate.

Cheesy Broccoli Gratin

Servings: 2

Cooking Time: 12 To 14 Minutes

Ingredients:

- ⅓ cup fat-free milk
- 1 tablespoon all-purpose or gluten-free flour
- ½ tablespoon olive oil
- ½ teaspoon ground sage
- ¼ teaspoon kosher salt
- ⅛ teaspoon freshly ground black pepper
- 2 cups roughly chopped broccoli florets
- 6 tablespoons shredded Cheddar cheese
- 2 tablespoons panko bread crumbs
- 1 tablespoon grated Parmesan cheese
- Olive oil spray

Directions:

1. Select BAKE, set the temperature to 330°F, and set the time to 14 minutes. Select START/STOP to begin preheating.
2. Spritz a baking pan with olive oil spray.
3. Mix the milk, flour, olive oil, sage, salt, and pepper in a medium bowl and whisk to combine. Stir in the broccoli florets, Cheddar cheese, bread crumbs, and Parmesan cheese and toss to coat.
4. Pour the broccoli mixture into the prepared baking pan. Place the pan directly in the pot.
5. Close the hood and BAKE for 12 to 14 minutes until the top is golden brown and the broccoli is tender.
6. Serve immediately.

Prosciutto Mini Mushroom Pizza

Servings: 3

Cooking Time: 5 Minutes

Ingredients:

- 3 portobello mushroom caps, cleaned and scooped
- 3 tablespoons olive oil
- Pinch of salt
- Pinch of dried Italian seasonings
- 3 tablespoons tomato sauce
- 3 tablespoons shredded Mozzarella cheese
- 12 slices prosciutto

Directions:

1. Insert the Crisper Basket and close the hood. Select AIR CRISP, set the temperature to 330°F, and set the time to 5 minutes. Select START/STOP to begin preheating.
2. Season both sides of the portobello mushrooms with a drizzle of olive oil, then sprinkle salt and the Italian seasonings on the insides.
3. With a knife, spread the tomato sauce evenly over the mushroom, before adding the Mozzarella on top.
4. Put the portobello in the Crisper Basket. Close the hood and AIR CRISP for 1 minutes, before taking the Crisper Basket out of the grill and putting the prosciutto slices on top. AIR CRISP for another 4 minutes.
5. Serve warm.

Flatbread Pizza

Servings: 4

Cooking Time: 10 Minutes

Ingredients:

- 1 (14-ounce) package refrigerated pizza dough
- 2 tablespoons extra-virgin olive oil
- ½ cup prepared Alfredo sauce
- 1 medium zucchini, cut into ⅛-inch-thick discs
- ½ cup fresh spinach
- ½ red onion, sliced
- 4 cherry tomatoes, sliced

Directions:

1. Insert the Grill Grate and close the hood. Select GRILL, set the temperature to MED, and set the time to 10 minutes. Select START/STOP to begin preheating.
2. While the unit is preheating, roll out the dough into a rectangle slightly smaller than the Grill Grate (8 by 11 inches). Brush the olive oil on both sides of the dough.
3. When the unit beeps to signify it has preheated, place the dough on the Grill Grate. Close the hood and grill for 5 minutes.
4. After 5 minutes, open the hood and flip the dough. (Or skip flipping, if you'd rather.) Spread the Alfredo sauce across the dough, leaving a 1-inch border. Layer the zucchini, spinach, red onion, and cherry tomatoes across the dough. Close the hood and cook for 5 minutes more.
5. When cooking is complete, remove the pizza from the grill. Slice and serve.

Loaded Zucchini Boats

Servings: 4

Cooking Time: 10 Minutes

Ingredients:

- 4 medium zucchini
- 1 cup panko bread crumbs
- 2 garlic cloves, minced
- ½ small white onion, diced
- ½ cup grated Parmesan cheese
- 1 tablespoon Italian seasoning

Directions:

1. Insert the Grill Grate and close the hood. Select GRILL, set the temperature to HI, and set the time to 10 minutes. Select START/STOP to begin preheating.
2. While the unit is preheating, cut the zucchini in half lengthwise. Carefully scoop out the flesh and put it in a medium bowl. Set the boats aside.
3. Add the panko bread crumbs, garlic, onion, Parmesan cheese, and Italian seasoning to the bowl and mix well. Spoon the filling into each zucchini half.
4. When the unit beeps to signify it has preheated, place the zucchini boats on the Grill Grate, cut-side up. Close the hood and grill for 10 minutes.
5. When cooking is complete, the cheese will be melted and the tops will be crispy and golden brown. Remove the zucchini boats from the grill and serve.

Honey-glazed Baby Carrots

Servings: 4

Cooking Time: 12 Minutes

Ingredients:

- 1 pound baby carrots
- 2 tablespoons olive oil
- 1 tablespoon honey
- 1 teaspoon dried dill
- Salt and black pepper, to taste

Directions:

1. Insert the Crisper Basket and close the hood. Select ROAST, set the temperature to 350°F, and set the time to 12 minutes. Select START/STOP to begin preheating.
2. Place the carrots in a large bowl. Add the olive oil, honey, dill, salt, and pepper and toss to coat well.
3. Arrange the carrots in the Crisper Basket. Close the hood and ROAST for 12 minutes, until crisp-tender. Shake the basket once during cooking.
4. Serve warm.

Mozzarella Broccoli Calzones

Servings: 4

Cooking Time: 24 Minutes

Ingredients:

- 1 head broccoli, trimmed into florets
- 2 tablespoons extra-virgin olive oil
- 1 store-bought pizza dough
- 2 to 3 tablespoons all-purpose flour, plus more for dusting
- 1 egg, beaten
- 2 cups shredded Mozzarella cheese
- 1 cup ricotta cheese
- ½ cup grated Parmesan cheese
- 1 garlic clove, grated
- Grated zest of 1 lemon
- ½ teaspoon red pepper flakes
- Cooking oil spray

Directions:

1. Insert the Crisper Basket and close the hood. Select AIR CRISP, set the temperature to 390°F, and set the time to 12 minutes. Select START/STOP to begin preheating.
2. Meanwhile, in a large bowl, toss the broccoli and olive oil until evenly coated.
3. When the unit beeps to signify it has preheated, add the broccoli to the basket. Close the hood and AIR CRISP for 6 minutes.
4. While the broccoli is cooking, divide the pizza dough into four equal pieces. Dust a clean work surface with the flour. Place the dough on the floured surface and roll each piece into an 8-inch round of even thickness. Dust your rolling pin and work surface with additional flour, as needed, to ensure the dough does not stick. Brush a thin coating of egg wash around the edges of each round.
5. After 6 minutes, shake the basket of broccoli. Place the basket back in the unit and close the hood to resume cooking.
6. Meanwhile, in a medium bowl, combine the Mozzarella, ricotta, Parmesan cheese, garlic, lemon zest, and red pepper flakes.
7. After cooking is complete, add the broccoli to the cheese mixture. Spoon one-quarter of the mixture onto one side of each dough. Fold the other half over the filling, and press firmly to seal the edges together. Brush each calzone all over with the remaining egg wash.
8. Select AIR CRISP, set the temperature to 390°F, and set the time to 12 minutes. Select START/STOP to begin preheating.
9. When the unit beeps to signify it has preheated, coat the Crisper Basket with cooking spray and place the calzones in the basket. AIR CRISP for 10 to 12 minutes, until golden brown.

Mascarpone Mushrooms

Servings: 4

Cooking Time: 15 Minutes

Ingredients:

- Vegetable oil spray
- 4 cups sliced mushrooms
- 1 medium yellow onion, chopped
- 2 cloves garlic, minced
- ¼ cup heavy whipping cream or half-and-half
- 8 ounces mascarpone cheese
- 1 teaspoon dried thyme
- 1 teaspoon kosher salt
- 1 teaspoon black pepper
- ½ teaspoon red pepper flakes
- 4 cups cooked konjac noodles, for serving
- ½ cup grated Parmesan cheese

Directions:

1. Select BAKE, set the temperature to 350°F, and set the time to 15 minutes. Select START/STOP to begin preheating.
2. Spray a heatproof pan with vegetable oil spray.
3. In a medium bowl, combine the mushrooms, onion, garlic, cream, mascarpone, thyme, salt, black pepper, and red pepper flakes. Stir to combine. Transfer the mixture to the prepared pan.
4. Place the pan directly in the pot. Close the hood and BAKE for 15 minutes, stirring halfway through the baking time.
5. Divide the pasta among four shallow bowls. Spoon the mushroom mixture evenly over the pasta. Sprinkle with Parmesan cheese and serve.

Crispy Noodle Vegetable Stir-fry

Servings: 4

Cooking Time: 20 Minutes

Ingredients:

- 4 cups water
- 3 (5-ounce) packages instant ramen noodles (flavor packets removed) or 1 (12-ounce) package chow mein noodles
- Extra-virgin olive oil, for drizzling, plus 3 tablespoons
- 3 garlic cloves, minced
- 3 teaspoons peeled minced fresh ginger
- 1 red bell pepper, cut into thin strips
- 4 ounces white mushrooms, sliced
- 1 (8-ounce) can sweet baby corn, drained
- 2 cups snap peas
- 2 cups broccoli florets
- 1 small carrot, diagonally sliced
- 1 cup vegetable broth
- 1 cup soy sauce
- ¼ cup rice vinegar
- 1 tablespoon sesame oil
- 3 tablespoons sugar
- 1 tablespoon cornstarch

Directions:

1. Insert the Cooking Pot and close the hood. Select GRILL, set the temperature to HI, and set the time to 20 minutes. Select START/STOP to begin preheating.
2. When the unit beeps to signify it has preheated, pour the water into the Cooking Pot and add the ramen noodles. Close the hood and cook for 5 minutes.
3. After 5 minutes, open the hood and remove the Cooking Pot. Drain the noodles and set aside. Insert the Grill Grate (along with the Cooking Pot). Make a large bed of noodles on the Grill Grate and drizzle olive oil over them. Close the hood and cook for 5 minutes. (If using chow mein noodles, flip them halfway through.)
4. After 5 minutes, the ramen noodles should be crispy and golden brown. Transfer the crispy noodles to a large serving plate.
5. Use grill mitts to remove the Grill Grate. To the Cooking Pot, add the remaining 3 tablespoons of olive oil and the garlic and ginger. Close the hood and cook for 2 minutes.
6. After 2 minutes, open the hood and add the red bell pepper, mushrooms, baby corn, snap peas, broccoli, and carrot. Close the hood and cook for 5 minutes.
7. While the vegetables are cooking, in a small bowl, combine the vegetable broth, soy sauce, vinegar, sesame oil, sugar, and cornstarch and mix until the sugar and cornstarch are dissolved.
8. After 5 minutes, open the hood, stir the vegetables, and add the broth mixture. Close the hood and cook for 3 minutes more.
9. When cooking is complete, open the hood and stir once more. Close the hood and let the vegetables sit in the pot for 3 minutes. Then, pour the vegetables and sauce on top of the crispy noodle bed and serve.

Sriracha Golden Cauliflower

Servings: 4

Cooking Time: 17 Minutes

Ingredients:

- ¼ cup vegan butter, melted
- ¼ cup sriracha sauce
- 4 cups cauliflower florets
- 1 cup bread crumbs
- 1 teaspoon salt

Directions:

1. Insert the Crisper Basket and close the hood. Select AIR CRISP, set the temperature to 375ºF, and set the time to 17 minutes. Select START/STOP to begin preheating.
2. Mix the sriracha and vegan butter in a bowl and pour this mixture over the cauliflower, taking care to cover each floret entirely.
3. In a separate bowl, combine the bread crumbs and salt.
4. Dip the cauliflower florets in the bread crumbs, coating each one well. Transfer to the basket. Close the hood and AIR CRISP for 17 minutes.
5. Serve hot.

Bean And Corn Stuffed Peppers

Servings: 6

Cooking Time: 32 Minutes

Ingredients:

- 6 red or green bell peppers, seeded, ribs removed, and top ½-inch cut off and reserved
- 4 garlic cloves, minced
- 1 small white onion, diced
- 2 bags instant rice, cooked in microwave
- 1 can red or green enchilada sauce
- ½ teaspoon chili powder
- ¼ teaspoon ground cumin
- ½ cup canned black beans, rinsed and drained
- ½ cup frozen corn
- ½ cup vegetable stock
- 1 bag shredded Colby Jack cheese, divided

Directions:

1. Chop the ½-inch portions of reserved bell pepper and place in a large mixing bowl. Add the garlic, onion, cooked instant rice, enchilada sauce, chili powder, cumin, black beans, corn, vegetable stock, and half the cheese. Mix to combine.
2. Use the cooking pot without the Grill Grate or Crisper Basket installed. Close the hood. Select ROAST, set the temperature to 350°F, and set the time to 32 minutes. Select START/STOP to begin preheating.
3. While the unit is preheating, spoon the mixture into the peppers, filling them up as full as possible. If necessary, lightly press the mixture down into the peppers to fit more in.
4. When the unit beeps to signify it has preheated, place the peppers, upright, in the pot. Close the hood and ROAST for 30 minutes.
5. After 30 minutes, sprinkle the remaining cheese over the top of the peppers. Close the hood and ROAST for the remaining 2 minutes.
6. When cooking is complete, serve immediately.

Grilled Vegetable Quesadillas

Servings: 4

Cooking Time: 8 Minutes

Ingredients:

- 1 medium onion, chopped
- 1 medium summer squash, halved lengthwise and thinly sliced into half-moons
- 1 medium zucchini, halved lengthwise and thinly sliced into half-moons
- Extra-virgin olive oil
- 4 (10-inch) flour tortillas
- 1 cup shredded mozzarella cheese
- ¼ cup chopped fresh cilantro (optional)

Directions:

1. Insert the Grill Grate and close the hood. Select GRILL, set the temperature to HI, and set the time to 8 minutes. Select START/STOP to begin preheating.
2. In a large bowl, combine the onion, summer squash, and zucchini and lightly coat with olive oil.
3. When the unit beeps to signify it has preheated, place the vegetables on the Grill Grate in a single layer. Close the hood and cook for 4 minutes.
4. While the vegetables are grilling, place the tortillas on a large tray and cover half of each with about ¼ cup of mozzarella.
5. After 4 minutes, open the hood and transfer the vegetables to the tortillas, evenly spreading on top of the cheese. Top the vegetables with the cilantro (if using). Fold the other half of each tortilla over to close. Place the quesadillas on the Grill Grate. Close the hood and cook for 2 minutes.
6. After 2 minutes, open the hood and flip the quesadillas. Close the hood and cook for 2 minutes more.
7. When cooking is complete, the cheese will be melted and the tortillas will be crispy. Remove the quesadillas from the grill and serve.

BBQ Grill & Smoker Cookbook

Crusted Brussels Sprouts With Sage

Servings: 4

Cooking Time: 15 Minutes

Ingredients:

- 1 pound Brussels sprouts, halved
- 1 cup bread crumbs
- 2 tablespoons grated Grana Padano cheese
- 1 tablespoon paprika
- 2 tablespoons canola oil
- 1 tablespoon chopped sage

Directions:

1. Line the Crisper Basket with parchment paper.
2. Insert the Crisper Basket and close the hood. Select ROAST, set the temperature to 400ºF, and set the time to 15 minutes. Select START/STOP to begin preheating.
3. In a small bowl, thoroughly mix the bread crumbs, cheese, and paprika. In a large bowl, place the Brussels sprouts and drizzle the canola oil over the top. Sprinkle with the bread crumb mixture and toss to coat.
4. Place the Brussels sprouts in the Crisper Basket. Close the hood and ROAST for 15 minutes, or until the Brussels sprouts are lightly browned and crisp. Shake the basket a few times during cooking to ensure even cooking.
5. Transfer the Brussels sprouts to a plate and sprinkle the sage on top before serving.

Fast And Easy Asparagus

Servings: 4

Cooking Time: 5 Minutes

Ingredients:

- 1 pound fresh asparagus spears, trimmed
- 1 tablespoon olive oil
- Salt and ground black pepper, to taste

Directions:

1. Insert the Crisper Basket and close the hood. Select AIR CRISP, set the temperature to 375ºF, and set the time to 5 minutes. Select START/STOP to begin preheating.
2. Combine all the ingredients and transfer to the Crisper Basket.
3. Close the hood and AIR CRISP for 5 minutes or until soft.
4. Serve hot.

Spicy Cauliflower Roast

Servings: 4

Cooking Time: 20 Minutes

Ingredients:

- Cauliflower:
- 5 cups cauliflower florets
- 3 tablespoons vegetable oil
- ½ teaspoon ground cumin
- ½ teaspoon ground coriander
- ½ teaspoon kosher salt
- Sauce:
- ½ cup Greek yogurt or sour cream
- ¼ cup chopped fresh cilantro
- 1 jalapeño, coarsely chopped
- 4 cloves garlic, peeled
- ½ teaspoon kosher salt
- 2 tablespoons water

Directions:

1. Insert the Crisper Basket and close the hood. Select ROAST, set the temperature to 400ºF, and set the time to 20 minutes. Select START/STOP to begin preheating.
2. In a large bowl, combine the cauliflower, oil, cumin, coriander, and salt. Toss to coat.
3. Put the cauliflower in the Crisper Basket. Close the hood and ROAST for 20 minutes, stirring halfway through the roasting time.
4. Meanwhile, in a blender, combine the yogurt, cilantro, jalapeño, garlic, and salt. Blend, adding the water as needed to keep the blades moving and to thin the sauce.
5. At the end of roasting time, transfer the cauliflower to a large serving bowl. Pour the sauce over and toss gently to coat. Serve immediately.

Black Bean And Tomato Chili

Servings: 6

Cooking Time: 23 Minutes

Ingredients:

- 1 tablespoon olive oil
- 1 medium onion, diced
- 3 garlic cloves, minced
- 1 cup vegetable broth
- 3 cans black beans, drained and rinsed
- 2 cans diced tomatoes
- 2 chipotle peppers, chopped
- 2 teaspoons cumin
- 2 teaspoons chili powder
- 1 teaspoon dried oregano
- ½ teaspoon salt

Directions:

1. Over a medium heat, fry the garlic and onions in the olive oil for 3 minutes.
2. Add the remaining ingredients, stirring constantly and scraping the bottom to prevent sticking.
3. Select BAKE, set the temperature to 400°F, and set the time to 20 minutes. Select START/STOP to begin preheating.
4. Take a baking pan and place the mixture inside. Put a sheet of aluminum foil on top.
5. Place the pan directly in the pot. Close the hood and BAKE for 20 minutes.
6. When ready, plate up and serve immediately.

Cheesy Macaroni Balls

Servings: 2

Cooking Time: 10 Minutes

Ingredients:

- 2 cups leftover macaroni
- 1 cup shredded Cheddar cheese
- ½ cup flour
- 1 cup bread crumbs
- 3 large eggs
- 1 cup milk
- ½ teaspoon salt
- ¼ teaspoon black pepper

Directions:

1. Insert the Crisper Basket and close the hood. Select AIR CRISP, set the temperature to 365°F, and set the time to 10 minutes. Select START/STOP to begin preheating.
2. In a bowl, combine the leftover macaroni and shredded cheese.
3. Pour the flour in a separate bowl. Put the bread crumbs in a third bowl. Finally, in a fourth bowl, mix the eggs and milk with a whisk.
4. With an ice-cream scoop, create balls from the macaroni mixture. Coat them the flour, then in the egg mixture, and lastly in the bread crumbs.
5. Arrange the balls in the basket. Close the hood and AIR CRISP for 10 minutes, giving them an occasional stir. Ensure they crisp up nicely.
6. Serve hot.

Simple Ratatouille

Servings: 2

Cooking Time: 16 Minutes

Ingredients:

- 2 Roma tomatoes, thinly sliced
- 1 zucchini, thinly sliced
- 2 yellow bell peppers, sliced
- 2 garlic cloves, minced
- 2 tablespoons olive oil
- 2 tablespoons herbes de Provence
- 1 tablespoon vinegar
- Salt and black pepper, to taste

Directions:

1. Select ROAST, set the temperature to 390°F, and set the time to 16 minutes. Select START/STOP to begin preheating.
2. Place the tomatoes, zucchini, bell peppers, garlic, olive oil, herbes de Provence, and vinegar in a large bowl and toss until the vegetables are evenly coated. Sprinkle with salt and pepper and toss again. Pour the vegetable mixture into the pot.
3. Close the hood and ROAST for 8 minutes. Stir and continue roasting for 8 minutes until tender.
4. Let the vegetable mixture stand for 5 minutes in the basket before removing and serving.

Vegetarian Meatballs

Servings: 3

Cooking Time: 18 Minutes

Ingredients:

- ½ cup grated carrots
- ½ cup sweet onions
- 2 tablespoons olive oil
- 1 cup rolled oats
- ½ cup roasted cashews
- 2 cups cooked chickpeas
- Juice of 1 lemon
- 2 tablespoons soy sauce
- 1 tablespoon flax meal
- 1 teaspoon garlic powder
- 1 teaspoon cumin
- ½ teaspoon turmeric

Directions:

1. Select ROAST, set the temperature to 350°F, and set the time to 6 minutes. Select START/STOP to begin preheating.
2. Mix together the carrots, onions, and olive oil in the pot and stir to combine.
3. Close the hood and ROAST for 6 minutes.
4. Meanwhile, put the oats and cashews in a food processor or blender and pulse until coarsely ground. Transfer the mixture to a large bowl. Add the chickpeas, lemon juice, and soy sauce to the food processor and pulse until smooth. Transfer the chickpea mixture to the bowl of oat and cashew mixture.
5. Remove the carrots and onions from the pot to the bowl of chickpea mixture. Add the flax meal, garlic powder, cumin, and turmeric and stir to incorporate.
6. Scoop tablespoon-sized portions of the veggie mixture and roll them into balls with your hands. Transfer the balls to the Crisper Basket in a single layer.
7. Increase the temperature to 370°F and BAKE for 12 minutes until golden through. Flip the balls halfway through the cooking time.
8. Serve warm.

Hearty Roasted Veggie Salad

Servings: 2

Cooking Time: 20 Minutes

Ingredients:

- 1 potato, chopped
- 1 carrot, sliced diagonally
- 1 cup cherry tomatoes
- ½ small beetroot, sliced
- ¼ onion, sliced
- ½ teaspoon turmeric
- ½ teaspoon cumin
- ¼ teaspoon sea salt
- 2 tablespoons olive oil, divided
- A handful of arugula
- A handful of baby spinach
- Juice of 1 lemon
- 3 tablespoons canned chickpeas, for serving
- Parmesan shavings, for serving

Directions:

1. Insert the Crisper Basket and close the hood. Select ROAST, set the temperature to 370°F, and set the time to 20 minutes. Select START/STOP to begin preheating.
2. Combine the potato, carrot, cherry tomatoes, beetroot, onion, turmeric, cumin, salt, and 1 tablespoon of olive oil in a large bowl and toss until well coated.
3. Arrange the veggies in the Crisper Basket. Close the hood and ROAST for 20 minutes, shaking the basket halfway through.
4. Let the veggies cool for 5 to 10 minutes in the basket.
5. Put the arugula, baby spinach, lemon juice, and remaining 1 tablespoon of olive oil in a salad bowl and stir to combine. Mix in the roasted veggies and toss well.
6. Scatter the chickpeas and Parmesan shavings on top and serve immediately.

Creamy Corn Casserole

Servings: 4

Cooking Time: 15 Minutes

Ingredients:

- 2 cups frozen yellow corn
- 1 egg, beaten
- 3 tablespoons flour
- ½ cup grated Swiss or Havarti cheese
- ½ cup light cream
- ¼ cup milk
- Pinch salt
- Freshly ground black pepper, to taste
- 2 tablespoons butter, cut into cubes
- Nonstick cooking spray

Directions:

1. Select BAKE, set the temperature to 320°F, and set the time to 15 minutes. Select START/STOP to begin preheating.
2. Spritz a baking pan with nonstick cooking spray.
3. Stir together the remaining ingredients except the butter in a medium bowl until well incorporated.
4. Transfer the mixture to the prepared baking pan and scatter with the butter cubes.
5. Place the pan directly in the pot. Close the hood and BAKE for 15 minutes, or until the top is golden brown and a toothpick inserted in the center comes out clean.
6. Let the casserole cool for 5 minutes before slicing into wedges and serving.

Corn Pakodas

Servings: 5

Cooking Time: 8 Minutes

Ingredients:

- 1 cup flour
- ¼ teaspoon baking soda
- ¼ teaspoon salt
- ½ teaspoon curry powder
- ½ teaspoon red chili powder
- ¼ teaspoon turmeric powder
- ¼ cup water
- 10 cobs baby corn, blanched
- Cooking spray

Directions:

1. Insert the Crisper Basket and close the hood. Select AIR CRISP, set the temperature to 425°F, and set the time to 8 minutes. Select START/STOP to begin preheating.
2. Cover the Crisper Basket with aluminum foil and spritz with the cooking spray.
3. In a bowl, combine all the ingredients, save for the corn. Stir with a whisk until well combined.
4. Coat the corn in the batter and put inside the basket.
5. Close the hood and AIR CRISP for 8 minutes until a golden brown color is achieved.
6. Serve hot.

Garlic Roasted Asparagus

Servings: 4

Cooking Time: 10 Minutes

Ingredients:

- 1 pound asparagus, woody ends trimmed
- 2 tablespoons olive oil
- 1 tablespoon balsamic vinegar
- 2 teaspoons minced garlic
- Salt and freshly ground black pepper, to taste

Directions:

1. Insert the Crisper Basket and close the hood. Select ROAST, set the temperature to 400°F, and set the time to 10 minutes. Select START/STOP to begin preheating.
2. In a large shallow bowl, toss the asparagus with the olive oil, balsamic vinegar, garlic, salt, and pepper until thoroughly coated.
3. Arrange the asparagus in the Crisper Basket. Close the hood and ROAST for 10 minutes until crispy. Flip the asparagus with tongs halfway through the cooking time.
4. Serve warm.

Grilled Mozzarella And Tomatoes

Servings: 4

Cooking Time: 5 Minutes

Ingredients:

- 4 large, round, firm tomatoes
- ½ cup Italian dressing
- 1 cup shredded mozzarella
- ½ cup chopped fresh basil, for garnish

Directions:

1. Insert the Grill Grate and close the hood. Select GRILL, set the temperature to HI, and set the time to 5 minutes. Select START/STOP to begin preheating.
2. While the unit is preheating, cut the tomatoes in half crosswise. Pour about 1 tablespoon of Italian dressing on each tomato half.
3. When the unit beeps to signify it has preheated, place the tomatoes on the Grill Grate, cut-side up. If the tomatoes won't stand upright, slice a small piece from the bottom to level them out. Close the hood and grill for 2 minutes.
4. After 2 minutes, open the hood and evenly distribute the mozzarella cheese on top of the tomatoes. Close the hood and cook for 3 minutes more, or until the cheese is melted.
5. When cooking is complete, remove the tomatoes from the grill. Garnish with the basil and serve.

Cashew Stuffed Mushrooms

Servings: 6

Cooking Time: 15 Minutes

Ingredients:

- 1 cup basil
- ½ cup cashew, soaked overnight
- ½ cup nutritional yeast
- 1 tablespoon lemon juice
- 2 cloves garlic
- 1 tablespoon olive oil
- Salt, to taste
- 1 pound baby bella mushroom, stems removed

Directions:

1. Insert the Crisper Basket and close the hood. Select AIR CRISP, set the temperature to 400ºF, and set the time to 15 minutes. Select START/STOP to begin preheating.
2. Prepare the pesto. In a food processor, blend the basil, cashew nuts, nutritional yeast, lemon juice, garlic and olive oil to combine well. Sprinkle with salt, as desired.
3. Turn the mushrooms cap-side down and spread the pesto on the underside of each cap.
4. Transfer to the basket. Close the hood and AIR CRISP for 15 minutes.
5. Serve warm.

Creamy And Cheesy Spinach

Servings: 4

Cooking Time: 15 Minutes

Ingredients:

- Vegetable oil spray
- 1 package frozen spinach, thawed and squeezed dry
- ½ cup chopped onion
- 2 cloves garlic, minced
- 4 ounces cream cheese, diced
- ½ teaspoon ground nutmeg
- 1 teaspoon kosher salt
- 1 teaspoon black pepper
- ½ cup grated Parmesan cheese

Directions:

1. Select BAKE, set the temperature to 350ºF, and set the time to 15 minutes. Select START/STOP to begin preheating.
2. Spray a heatproof pan with vegetable oil spray.
3. In a medium bowl, combine the spinach, onion, garlic, cream cheese, nutmeg, salt, and pepper. Transfer to the prepared pan.
4. Place the pan directly in the pot. Close the hood and BAKE for 10 minutes. Open and stir to thoroughly combine the cream cheese and spinach.
5. Sprinkle the Parmesan cheese on top. Bake for 5 minutes, or until the cheese has melted and browned.
6. Serve hot.

Meats

Meats

Garlic Herb Crusted Lamb

Servings: 6

Cooking Time: 1 Hour

Ingredients:

- ¼ cup red wine vinegar
- 3 garlic cloves, minced
- 1 tablespoon garlic powder
- 1 tablespoon paprika
- 1 tablespoon ground cumin
- 1 tablespoon dried parsley
- 1 tablespoon dried thyme
- 1 tablespoon dried oregano
- 1 teaspoon salt
- ½ teaspoon freshly ground black pepper
- Juice of ½ lemon
- 1 (3-pound) boneless leg of lamb

Directions:

1. In a large bowl, mix together the vinegar, garlic, garlic powder, paprika, cumin, parsley, thyme, oregano, salt, pepper, and lemon juice until well combined—the marinade will turn into a thick paste. Add the leg of lamb and massage the marinade into the meat. Coat the lamb with the marinade and let sit for at least 30 minutes. If marinating for longer, cover and refrigerate.
2. Plug the thermometer into the unit. Insert the Grill Grate and close the hood. Select GRILL, set the temperature to LO, and set the time to 30 minutes. Insert the Smart Thermometer into the thickest part of the meat. Select START/STOP to begin preheating.
3. When the unit beeps to signify it has preheated, place the lamb on the Grill Grate. Select the BEEF/LAMB preset and choose MEDIUM-WELL or according to your desired doneness. Close the hood and cook for 30 minutes.
4. After 30 minutes, which is the maximum time for the LO setting, select GRILL again, set the temperature to LO, and set the time to 30 minutes. Select START/STOP and press PREHEAT to skip preheating. Cook until the Smart Thermometer indicates that the desired internal temperature has been reached.
5. When cooking is complete, remove the lamb from the grill and serve.

Spaghetti Squash Lasagna

Servings: 6

Cooking Time: 1 Hour 15 Minutes

Ingredients:

- 2 large spaghetti squash, cooked
- 4 pounds ground beef
- 1 large jar Marinara sauce
- 25 slices Mozzarella cheese
- 30 ounces whole-milk ricotta cheese

Directions:

1. Select BAKE, set the temperature to 375°F, and set the time to 45 minutes. Select START/STOP to begin preheating.
2. Slice the spaghetti squash and place it face down inside a baking pan. Fill with water until covered.
3. Place the pan directly in the pot. Close the hood and BAKE for 45 minutes until skin is soft.
4. Sear the ground beef in a skillet over medium-high heat for 5 minutes or until browned, then add the marinara sauce and heat until warm. Set aside.
5. Scrape the flesh off the cooked squash to resemble strands of spaghetti.
6. Layer the lasagna in a large greased pan in alternating layers of spaghetti squash, beef sauce, Mozzarella, ricotta. Repeat until all the ingredients have been used.
7. Place the pan directly in the pot. Close the hood and BAKE for 30 minutes.
8. Serve.

Bacon-wrapped Scallops

Servings: 4

Cooking Time: 10 Minutes

Ingredients:

- 8 slices bacon, cut in half
- 16 sea scallops, patted dry
- Cooking spray
- Salt and freshly ground black pepper, to taste
- 16 toothpicks, soaked in water for at least 30 minutes

Directions:

1. Insert the Crisper Basket and close the hood. Select AIR CRISP, set the temperature to 370ºF, and set the time to 10 minutes. Select START/STOP to begin preheating.
2. On a clean work surface, wrap half of a slice of bacon around each scallop and secure with a toothpick.
3. Lay the bacon-wrapped scallops in the Crisper Basket in a single layer. You may need to work in batches to avoid overcrowding.
4. Spritz the scallops with cooking spray and sprinkle the salt and pepper to season.
5. Close the hood and AIR CRISP for 10 minutes, flipping the scallops halfway through, or until the bacon is cooked through and the scallops are firm.
6. Remove the scallops from the basket to a plate and repeat with the remaining scallops. Serve warm.

Spicy Pork With Candy Onions

Servings: 4

Cooking Time: 52 Minutes

Ingredients:

- 2 teaspoons sesame oil
- 1 teaspoon dried sage, crushed
- 1 teaspoon cayenne pepper
- 1 rosemary sprig, chopped
- 1 thyme sprig, chopped
- Sea salt and ground black pepper, to taste
- 2 pounds pork leg roast, scored
- ½ pound candy onions, sliced
- 4 cloves garlic, finely chopped
- 2 chili peppers, minced

Directions:

1. Select AIR CRISP, set the temperature to 400ºF, and set the time to 52 minutes. Select START/STOP to begin preheating.
2. In a mixing bowl, combine the sesame oil, sage, cayenne pepper, rosemary, thyme, salt and black pepper until well mixed. In another bowl, place the pork leg and brush with the seasoning mixture.
3. Place the seasoned pork leg in a baking pan. Place the pan directly in the pot. Close the hood and AIR CRISP for 40 minutes, or until lightly browned, flipping halfway through. Add the candy onions, garlic and chili peppers to the pan and AIR CRISP for another 12 minutes.
4. Transfer the pork leg to a plate. Let cool for 5 minutes and slice. Spread the juices left in the pan over the pork and serve warm with the candy onions.

Cheesy Beef Meatballs

Servings: 6

Cooking Time: 18 Minutes

Ingredients:

- 1 pound ground beef
- ½ cup grated Parmesan cheese
- 1 tablespoon minced garlic
- ½ cup Mozzarella cheese
- 1 teaspoon freshly ground pepper

Directions:

1. Insert the Crisper Basket and close the hood. Select AIR CRISP, set the temperature to 400ºF, and set the time to 18 minutes. Select START/STOP to begin preheating.
2. In a bowl, mix all the ingredients together.
3. Roll the meat mixture into 5 generous meatballs. Transfer to the basket.
4. Close the hood and AIR CRISP for 18 minutes.
5. Serve immediately.

Sweet And Tangy Beef

Servings: 4

Cooking Time: 12 Minutes

Ingredients:

- For the beef
- 2 pounds top sirloin steak, thinly sliced
- 1 tablespoon cornstarch
- 3 tablespoons avocado oil
- 3 tablespoons soy sauce
- 2 tablespoons oyster sauce
- 1 tablespoon peeled minced fresh ginger
- 1 tablespoon sesame oil
- ½ teaspoon salt
- 1 onion, coarsely chopped
- 1 red bell pepper, coarsely chopped
- For the sweet and tangy sauce
- ½ cup water
- 2 tablespoons ketchup
- 2 tablespoons oyster sauce
- 2 tablespoons light brown sugar, packed
- 1 teaspoon salt
- 1 teaspoon sesame oil
- 1 tablespoon white vinegar
- 1 tablespoon Worcestershire sauce

Directions:

1. Insert the Cooking Pot and close the hood. Select GRILL, set the temperature to HI, and set the time to 12 minutes. Select START/STOP to begin preheating.
2. In a large bowl, combine the beef, cornstarch, avocado oil, soy sauce, oyster sauce, ginger, sesame oil, and salt. Mix well so the beef slices are fully coated.
3. When the unit beeps to signify it has preheated, transfer the beef to the Cooking Pot. Close the hood and cook for 6 minutes.
4. While the beef is cooking, in a small bowl, combine the water, ketchup, oyster sauce, brown sugar, salt, sesame oil, vinegar, and Worcestershire sauce. Stir until the sugar is dissolved.
5. After 6 minutes, open the hood and stir the beef. Add the onion and red bell pepper to the Cooking Pot. Close the hood and cook for 2 minutes. After 2 minutes, open the hood and add the sauce to the pot. Close the hood and cook for 4 minutes more.
6. When cooking is complete, spoon the beef and sauce over white rice, if desired. Serve.

Spicy Beef Lettuce Wraps

Servings: 4

Cooking Time: 10 Minutes

Ingredients:

- 1 pound ground beef
- 1 tablespoon sesame oil
- 1 tablespoon minced garlic
- 1 teaspoon peeled minced fresh ginger
- 3 tablespoons light brown sugar, packed
- ¼ cup soy sauce
- 1 teaspoon salt
- ½ teaspoon freshly ground black pepper
- 2 teaspoons sriracha
- 1 red chile, thinly sliced, or ¼ teaspoon red pepper flakes
- ½ cup sliced scallions, both white and green parts
- 12 butter lettuce leaves

Directions:

1. Insert the Cooking Pot and close the hood. Select GRILL, set the temperature to HI, and set the time to 10 minutes. Select START/STOP to begin preheating.
2. When the unit beeps to signify it has preheated, place the ground beef in the Cooking Pot. Carefully break the ground beef apart with a wooden spoon or spatula. Stir in the sesame oil, garlic, and ginger. Close the hood and cook for 5 minutes.
3. After 5 minutes, open the hood and stir the ground beef. Stir in the brown sugar, soy sauce, salt, pepper, and sriracha. Close the hood and cook for 5 minutes more.
4. When cooking is complete, open the hood and stir in the chile and scallions. Close the hood and let sit for about 3 minutes for the mixture to set.
5. Scoop the ground beef mixture into the lettuce leaves and serve.

Carne Asada Tacos

Servings: 4

Cooking Time: 15 Minutes

Ingredients:

- For the tacos
- ¼ cup avocado oil
- ¼ cup soy sauce
- ¼ cup orange juice
- 3 tablespoons white wine vinegar
- 3 tablespoons minced garlic
- Juice of 2 limes
- 1 teaspoon ground cumin
- 1 teaspoon salt
- 1 teaspoon freshly ground black pepper
- 1 teaspoon onion powder
- ½ cup chopped fresh cilantro
- 2 pounds skirt steak at least 1 inch thick
- 10 corn tortillas
- For the creamy cilantro sauce
- ¼ cup mayonnaise
- ¼ cup sour cream
- ¼ cup minced fresh cilantro, including stems
- Juice of 1 lime wedge, or more as desired
- ¼ teaspoon paprika
- ¼ teaspoon onion powder

Directions:

1. In a large bowl, whisk together the avocado oil, soy sauce, orange juice, vinegar, garlic, lime juice, cumin, salt, pepper, onion powder, and cilantro. Add the steak, making sure it is fully coated with the marinade. Set aside to marinate for 15 minutes.
2. Plug the thermometer into the unit. Insert the Grill Grate and close the hood. Select GRILL, set the temperature to HI, then select PRESET. Use the arrows to the right to select BEEF, then choose desired doneness. Insert the Smart Thermometer into the thickest part of the steak. Select START/STOP to begin preheating.
3. When the unit beeps to signify it has preheated, place the steak on the Grill Grate. Close the hood to begin cooking. The Foodi™ Grill will tell you when to flip the steak and when the desired internal temperature has been reached (15 minutes is for well-done steak).
4. While the steak is cooking, in a small bowl, combine the mayonnaise, sour cream, cilantro, lime juice, paprika, and onion powder.
5. When cooking is complete, remove the steak from the grill. Let it rest for 10 minutes before slicing against the grain. Serve in the tortillas and dress with the creamy cilantro sauce.

Crispy Pork Tenderloin

Servings: 6

Cooking Time: 10 Minutes

Ingredients:

- 2 large egg whites
- 1½ tablespoons Dijon mustard
- 2 cups crushed pretzel crumbs
- 1½ pounds pork tenderloin, cut into ¼-pound sections
- Cooking spray

Directions:

1. Spritz the Crisper Basket with cooking spray.
2. Insert the Crisper Basket and close the hood. Select AIR CRISP, set the temperature to 350°F, and set the time to 10 minutes. Select START/STOP to begin preheating.
3. Whisk the egg whites with Dijon mustard in a bowl until bubbly. Pour the pretzel crumbs in a separate bowl.
4. Dredge the pork tenderloin in the egg white mixture and press to coat. Shake the excess off and roll the tenderloin over the pretzel crumbs.
5. Arrange the well-coated pork tenderloin in batches in a single layer in the Crisper Basket and spritz with cooking spray.
6. Close the hood and AIR CRISP for 10 minutes or until the pork is golden brown and crispy. Flip the pork halfway through. Repeat with remaining pork sections.
7. Serve immediately.

BBQ Grill & Smoker Cookbook

Herb And Pesto Stuffed Pork Loin

Servings: 8

Cooking Time: 15 Minutes

Ingredients:

- 1 (4-pound) boneless center-cut pork loin
- ½ cup avocado oil
- ½ cup grated Parmesan cheese
- 2 tablespoons finely chopped fresh basil
- 1 tablespoon finely chopped fresh parsley
- 1 tablespoon chopped fresh chives
- ½ teaspoon finely chopped fresh rosemary
- 5 garlic cloves, minced

Directions:

1. Butterfly the pork loin. You can use the same method as you would for a chicken breast or steak (see here), but because a pork loin is thicker, you can perform this double butterfly technique: Place the boneless, trimmed loin on a cutting board. One-third from the bottom of the loin, slice horizontally from the side (parallel to the cutting board), stopping about ½ inch from the opposite side, and open the flap like a book. Make another horizontal cut from the thicker side of the loin to match the thickness of the first cut, stopping again ½ inch from the edge. Open up the flap to create a rectangular piece of flat meat.
2. Plug the thermometer into the unit. Insert the Grill Grate and close the hood. Select GRILL, set the temperature to MED, and select PRESET. Use the arrows to the right to select PORK. The unit will default to WELL to cook pork to a safe temperature. Select START/STOP to begin preheating.
3. While the unit is preheating, in a small bowl, combine the avocado oil, Parmesan cheese, basil, parsley, chives, rosemary, and garlic. Spread the pesto sauce evenly over the cut side of each tenderloin. Starting from a longer side, roll up the pork tightly over the filling. Use toothpicks to secure the ends. Insert the Smart Thermometer into the thickest part of the meat.
4. When the unit beeps to signify it has preheated, place the loin on the Grill Grate. Close the hood to begin cooking.
5. When the Foodi™ Grill indicates it's time to flip, open the hood and flip the loin. Close the hood to continue cooking.
6. When cooking is complete, the Smart Thermometer will indicate that the internal temperature has been reached. Open the hood and remove the loin. Let the meat rest for 10 minutes before slicing in between the toothpicks. Serve.

Bacon Burger Meatballs

Servings: 4

Cooking Time: 20 Minutes

Ingredients:

- 1 white onion, diced
- 1 pound thick-cut bacon (12 to 16 slices), cooked and crumbled
- 8 ounces cream cheese, at room temperature
- 4 tablespoons minced garlic
- ¼ cup ketchup
- ¼ cup yellow mustard
- ¼ cup gluten-free Worcestershire sauce
- 3 eggs
- 2 pounds ground beef

Directions:

1. In a large bowl, mix together the onion, bacon crumbles, cream cheese, garlic, ketchup, mustard, Worcestershire sauce, and eggs. Add the ground beef and, using your hands, mix the ingredients together until just combined, being careful to not overmix. Form the mixture into 1½- to 2-inch meatballs. This should make 20 to 22 meatballs.
2. Insert the Grill Grate and close the hood. Select GRILL, set the temperature to MED, and set the time to 20 minutes. Select START/STOP to begin preheating.
3. When the unit beeps to signify it has preheated, place the meatballs on the Grill Grate. Close the hood and cook for 10 minutes.
4. After 10 minutes, open the hood and flip the meatballs. Close the hood and cook for 10 minutes more.
5. When cooking is complete, remove the meatballs from the grill and serve.

Teriyaki Pork And Mushroom Rolls

Servings: 6

Cooking Time: 8 Minutes

Ingredients:

- 4 tablespoons brown sugar
- 4 tablespoons mirin
- 4 tablespoons soy sauce
- 1 teaspoon almond flour
- 2-inch ginger, chopped
- 6 pork belly slices
- 6 ounces Enoki mushrooms

Directions:

1. Mix the brown sugar, mirin, soy sauce, almond flour, and ginger together until brown sugar dissolves.
2. Take pork belly slices and wrap around a bundle of mushrooms. Brush each roll with teriyaki sauce. Chill for half an hour.
3. Insert the Crisper Basket and close the hood. Select AIR CRISP, set the temperature to 350ºF, and set the time to 8 minutes. Select START/STOP to begin preheating.
4. Add marinated pork rolls to the basket.
5. Close the hood and AIR CRISP for 8 minutes. Flip the rolls halfway through.
6. Serve immediately.

Vietnamese Pork Chops

Servings: 2

Cooking Time: 12 Minutes

Ingredients:

- 1 tablespoon chopped shallot
- 1 tablespoon chopped garlic
- 1 tablespoon fish sauce
- 3 tablespoons lemongrass
- 1 teaspoon soy sauce
- 1 tablespoon brown sugar
- 1 tablespoon olive oil
- 1 teaspoon ground black pepper
- 2 pork chops

Directions:

1. Combine shallot, garlic, fish sauce, lemongrass, soy sauce, brown sugar, olive oil, and pepper in a bowl. Stir to mix well.
2. Put the pork chops in the bowl. Toss to coat well. Place the bowl in the refrigerator to marinate for 2 hours.
3. Insert the Crisper Basket and close the hood. Select AIR CRISP, set the temperature to 400ºF, and set the time to 12 minutes. Select START/STOP to begin preheating.
4. Remove the pork chops from the bowl and discard the marinade. Transfer the chops into the basket.
5. Close the hood and AIR CRISP for 12 minutes or until lightly browned. Flip the pork chops halfway through the cooking time.
6. Remove the pork chops from the basket and serve hot.

Barbecue Pork Ribs

Servings: 4

Cooking Time: 30 Minutes

Ingredients:

- 1 tablespoon barbecue dry rub
- 1 teaspoon mustard
- 1 tablespoon apple cider vinegar
- 1 teaspoon sesame oil
- 1 pound pork ribs, chopped

Directions:

1. Combine the dry rub, mustard, apple cider vinegar, and sesame oil, then coat the ribs with this mixture. Refrigerate the ribs for 20 minutes.
2. Insert the Crisper Basket and close the hood. Select AIR CRISP, set the temperature to 360ºF, and set the time to 30 minutes. Select START/STOP to begin preheating.
3. When the ribs are ready, place them in the basket. Close the hood and AIR CRISP for 15 minutes. Flip them and AIR CRISP on the other side for a further 15 minutes.
4. Serve immediately.

Rack Of Lamb Chops With Rosemary

Servings: 2

Cooking Time: 14 Minutes

Ingredients:

- 3 tablespoons extra-virgin olive oil
- 1 garlic clove, minced
- 1 tablespoon fresh rosemary, chopped
- ½ rack lamb
- Sea salt, to taste
- Freshly ground black pepper, to taste

Directions:

1. Combine the oil, garlic, and rosemary in a large bowl. Season the rack of lamb with the salt and pepper, then place the lamb in the bowl, using tongs to turn and coat fully in the oil mixture. Cover and refrigerate for 2 hours.
2. Insert the Grill Grate and close the hood. Select GRILL, set the temperature to HIGH, and set the time to 14 minutes. Select START/STOP to begin preheating.
3. When the unit beeps to signify it has preheated, place the lamb on the Grill Grate. Close the hood and GRILL for 6 minutes. After 6 minutes, flip the lamb and continue grilling for 6 minutes more.
4. Cooking is complete when the internal temperature of the lamb reaches 145ºF on a food thermometer. If needed, GRILL for up to 2 minutes more.

Smoked Beef

Servings: 8

Cooking Time: 45 Minutes

Ingredients:

- 2 pounds roast beef, at room temperature
- 2 tablespoons extra-virgin olive oil
- 1 teaspoon sea salt flakes
- 1 teaspoon ground black pepper
- 1 teaspoon smoked paprika
- Few dashes of liquid smoke
- 2 jalapeño peppers, thinly sliced

Directions:

1. Select ROAST, set the temperature to 330ºF, and set the time to 45 minutes. Select START/STOP to begin preheating.
2. With kitchen towels, pat the beef dry.
3. Massage the extra-virgin olive oil, salt, black pepper, and paprika into the meat. Cover with liquid smoke.
4. Put the beef in the pot. Close the hood and ROAST for 30 minutes. Flip the roast over and allow to roast for another 15 minutes.
5. When cooked through, serve topped with sliced jalapeños.

Homemade Teriyaki Pork Ribs

Servings: 4

Cooking Time: 30 Minutes

Ingredients:

- ¼ cup soy sauce
- ¼ cup honey
- 1 teaspoon garlic powder
- 1 teaspoon ground dried ginger
- 4 boneless country-style pork ribs
- Cooking spray

Directions:

1. Spritz the Crisper Basket with cooking spray.
2. Insert the Crisper Basket and close the hood. Select AIR CRISP, set the temperature to 350ºF, and set the time to 30 minutes. Select START/STOP to begin preheating.
3. Make the teriyaki sauce: combine the soy sauce, honey, garlic powder, and ginger in a bowl. Stir to mix well.
4. Brush the ribs with half of the teriyaki sauce, then arrange the ribs in the basket. Spritz with cooking spray. You may need to work in batches to avoid overcrowding.
5. Close the hood and AIR CRISP for 30 minutes or until the internal temperature of the ribs reaches at least 145ºF. Brush the ribs with remaining teriyaki sauce and flip halfway through.
6. Serve immediately.

Citrus Carnitas

Servings: 6

Cooking Time: 25 Minutes

Ingredients:

- 2½ pounds boneless country-style pork ribs, cut into 2-inch pieces
- 3 tablespoons olive brine
- 1 tablespoon minced fresh oregano leaves
- ⅓ cup orange juice
- 1 teaspoon ground cumin
- 1 tablespoon minced garlic
- 1 teaspoon salt
- 1 teaspoon ground black pepper
- Cooking spray

Directions:

1. Combine all the ingredients in a large bowl. Toss to coat the pork ribs well. Wrap the bowl in plastic and refrigerate for at least an hour to marinate.
2. Spritz the Crisper Basket with cooking spray.
3. Insert the Crisper Basket and close the hood. Select AIR CRISP, set the temperature to 400°F, and set the time to 25 minutes. Select START/STOP to begin preheating.
4. Arrange the marinated pork ribs in a single layer in the basket and spritz with cooking spray.
5. Close the hood and AIR CRISP for 25 minutes or until well browned. Flip the ribs halfway through.
6. Serve immediately.

Italian Sausage And Peppers

Servings: 4

Cooking Time: 10 Minutes

Ingredients:

- 1 green bell pepper
- 1 large red onion
- 1 pound ground Italian sausage (not links)
- 1 tablespoon garlic, minced
- 2 tablespoons white wine vinegar

Directions:

1. Insert the Cooking Pot and close the hood. Select GRILL, set the temperature to HI, and set the time to 10 minutes. Select START/STOP to begin preheating.
2. While the unit is preheating, cut the bell pepper into strips and slice the red onion.
3. When the unit beeps to signify it has preheated, place the sausage, garlic, and vinegar in the Cooking Pot. Slowly break apart the sausage using a wooden spoon or a spatula. Close the hood and cook for 5 minutes.
4. After 5 minutes, open the hood and stir the sausage. Add the bell pepper and onion. Close the hood and cook for 5 minutes more.
5. When cooking is complete, stir the sausage, pepper, and onion again. Serve.

Mozzarella Meatball Sandwiches With Basil

Servings: 4

Cooking Time: 10 Minutes

Ingredients:

- 12 frozen meatballs
- 8 slices Mozzarella cheese
- 4 sub rolls, halved lengthwise
- ½ cup marinara sauce, warmed
- 12 fresh basil leaves

Directions:

1. Insert the Crisper Basket and close the hood. Select AIR CRISP, set the temperature to 350°F, and set the time to 10 minutes. Select START/STOP to begin preheating.
2. When the unit beeps to signify it has preheated, place the meatballs in the basket. Close the hood and AIR CRISP for 5 minutes.
3. After 5 minutes, shake the basket of meatballs. Place the basket back in the unit and close the hood to resume cooking.
4. While the meatballs are cooking, place two slices of Mozzarella cheese on each sub roll. Use a spoon to spread the marinara sauce on top of the cheese slices. Press three leaves of basil into the sauce on each roll.
5. When cooking is complete, place three meatballs on each sub roll. Serve immediately.

Pork Sausage With Cauliflower Mash

Servings: 6

Cooking Time: 27 Minutes

Ingredients:

- 1 pound cauliflower, chopped
- 6 pork sausages, chopped
- ½ onion, sliced
- 3 eggs, beaten
- ⅓ cup Colby cheese
- 1 teaspoon cumin powder
- ½ teaspoon tarragon
- ½ teaspoon sea salt
- ½ teaspoon ground black pepper
- Cooking spray

Directions:

1. Select BAKE, set the temperature to 365°F, and set the time to 27 minutes. Select START/STOP to begin preheating.
2. Spritz a baking pan with cooking spray.
3. In a saucepan over medium heat, boil the cauliflower until tender. Place the boiled cauliflower in a food processor and pulse until puréed. Transfer to a large bowl and combine with remaining ingredients until well blended.
4. Pour the cauliflower and sausage mixture into the baking pan. Place the pan directly in the pot. Close the hood and BAKE for 27 minutes, or until lightly browned.
5. Divide the mixture among six serving dishes and serve warm.

Easy Beef Schnitzel

Servings: 1

Cooking Time: 12 Minutes

Ingredients:

- ½ cup friendly bread crumbs
- 2 tablespoons olive oil
- Pepper and salt, to taste
- 1 egg, beaten
- 1 thin beef schnitzel

Directions:

1. Insert the Crisper Basket and close the hood. Select AIR CRISP, set the temperature to 350°F, and set the time to 12 minutes. Select START/STOP to begin preheating.
2. In a shallow dish, combine the bread crumbs, oil, pepper, and salt.
3. In a second shallow dish, place the beaten egg.
4. Dredge the schnitzel in the egg before rolling it in the bread crumbs.
5. Put the coated schnitzel in the Crisper Basket. Close the hood and AIR CRISP for 12 minutes. Flip the schnitzel halfway through.
6. Serve immediately.

Lamb Ribs With Fresh Mint

Servings: 4

Cooking Time: 18 Minutes

Ingredients:

- 2 tablespoons mustard
- 1 pound lamb ribs
- 1 teaspoon rosemary, chopped
- Salt and ground black pepper, to taste
- ¼ cup mint leaves, chopped
- 1 cup Greek yogurt

Directions:

1. Insert the Crisper Basket and close the hood. Select AIR CRISP, set the temperature to 350°F, and set the time to 18 minutes. Select START/STOP to begin preheating.
2. Use a brush to apply the mustard to the lamb ribs, and season with rosemary, salt, and pepper. Transfer to the basket.
3. Close the hood and AIR CRISP for 18 minutes.
4. Meanwhile, combine the mint leaves and yogurt in a bowl.
5. Remove the lamb ribs from the grill when cooked and serve with the mint yogurt.

Uncle's Famous Tri-tip

Servings: 6 To 8

Cooking Time: 20 Minutes

Ingredients:

- ¼ cup avocado oil
- ½ cup red wine vinegar
- ¼ cup light brown sugar, packed
- 4 tablespoons honey mustard
- 1 tablespoon garlic powder
- 1 tablespoon onion powder
- 1 tablespoon paprika
- 1 tablespoon salt
- 1 tablespoon freshly ground black pepper
- 3 pounds tri-tip

Directions:

1. In a large resealable bag, combine the avocado oil, red wine vinegar, brown sugar, honey mustard, garlic powder, onion powder, paprika, salt, and pepper. Add the tri-tip, seal, and massage the mixture into the meat. Refrigerate overnight.
2. About 20 minutes before grilling, remove the bag from the refrigerator so the marinade becomes liquid again at room temperature.
3. Plug the thermometer into the unit. Insert the Grill Grate and close the hood. Select GRILL, set the temperature to MED, and select PRESET. Use the arrows to the right to select BEEF, then choose desired doneness. Insert the Smart Thermometer into the thickest part of the meat. Select START/STOP to begin preheating.
4. When the unit beeps to signify it has preheated, place the tri-tip on the Grill Grate, fat-side up. Close the hood to begin cooking.
5. When the Foodi™ Grill indicates it is time to flip, open the hood and flip the tri-tip. Close the hood and continue cooking until the Smart Thermometer indicates your desired internal temperature has been reached.
6. When cooking is complete, remove the tri-tip from the grill. Let rest for 10 minutes before slicing against the grain. Serve.

Apple-glazed Pork

Servings: 4

Cooking Time: 19 Minutes

Ingredients:

- 1 sliced apple
- 1 small onion, sliced
- 2 tablespoons apple cider vinegar, divided
- ½ teaspoon thyme
- ½ teaspoon rosemary
- ¼ teaspoon brown sugar
- 3 tablespoons olive oil, divided
- ¼ teaspoon smoked paprika
- 4 pork chops
- Salt and ground black pepper, to taste

Directions:

1. Select BAKE, set the temperature to 350°F, and set the time to 4 minutes. Select START/STOP to begin preheating.
2. Combine the apple slices, onion, 1 tablespoon of vinegar, thyme, rosemary, brown sugar, and 2 tablespoons of olive oil in a baking pan. Stir to mix well.
3. Place the pan directly in the pot. Close the hood and BAKE for 4 minutes.
4. Meanwhile, combine the remaining vinegar and olive oil, and paprika in a large bowl. Sprinkle with salt and ground black pepper. Stir to mix well. Dredge the pork in the mixture and toss to coat well.
5. Remove the baking pan from the grill and put in the pork. Place the pan directly in the pot. Close the hood and AIR CRISP for 10 minutes to lightly brown the pork. Flip the pork chops halfway through.
6. Remove the pork from the grill and baste with baked apple mixture on both sides. Put the pork back to the grill and AIR CRISP for an additional 5 minutes. Flip halfway through.
7. Serve immediately.

BBQ Grill & Smoker Cookbook

Grilled Pork Banh Mi

Servings: 6

Cooking Time: 15 Minutes

Ingredients:

- 3 tablespoons light brown sugar, packed
- 1 tablespoon soy sauce
- 3 tablespoons minced garlic
- Juice of 2 limes
- 1 shallot, finely minced
- 2 pounds pork tenderloin, cut into 1-inch-thick slices
- 1 daikon radish, cut into thin strips
- 1 large carrot, cut into thin strips
- 3 tablespoons rice vinegar
- ½ teaspoon kosher salt
- 1 teaspoon granulated sugar
- 6 sandwich-size baguettes
- Mayonnaise
- 1 cucumber, thinly sliced
- Fresh cilantro
- 1 jalapeño, sliced

Directions:

1. In a large bowl, combine the brown sugar, soy sauce, garlic, lime juice, shallot, and pork tenderloin slices. Marinate for at least 30 minutes. If marinating for longer, cover and refrigerate.
2. Insert the Cooking Pot and close the hood. Select GRILL, set the temperature to HI, and set the time to 15 minutes. Select START/STOP to begin preheating.
3. While the unit is preheating, in a medium bowl, combine the daikon, carrot, rice vinegar, salt, and sugar.
4. When the unit beeps to signify it has preheated, place the pork in the Cooking Pot. Feel free to add a little bit of the marinade to the pot. Close the hood and cook for 8 minutes.
5. After 8 minutes, open the hood and stir the pork. Close the hood and cook for 7 minutes more.
6. When cooking is complete, slice open each baguette and spread mayonnaise on both sides. Add a layer each of pork, pickled daikon and carrot, cucumber, cilantro, and jalapeño slices and serve.

Pork Chops In Bourbon

Servings: 4

Cooking Time: 35 Minutes

Ingredients:

- 2 cups ketchup
- ¾ cup bourbon
- ¼ cup apple cider vinegar
- ¼ cup soy sauce
- 1 cup packed brown sugar
- 3 tablespoons Worcestershire sauce
- ½ tablespoon dry mustard powder
- 4 boneless pork chops
- Sea salt, to taste
- Freshly ground black pepper, to taste

Directions:

1. In a medium saucepan over high heat, combine the ketchup, bourbon, vinegar, soy sauce, sugar, Worcestershire sauce, and mustard powder. Stir to combine and bring to a boil.
2. Reduce the heat to low and simmer, uncovered and stirring occasionally, for 20 minutes. The barbecue sauce will thicken while cooking. Once thickened, remove the pan from the heat and set aside.
3. While the barbecue sauce is cooking, insert the Grill Grate into the unit and close the hood. Select GRILL, set the temperature to MEDIUM, and set the time to 15 minutes. Select START/STOP to begin preheating.
4. When the unit beeps to signify it has preheated, place the pork chops on the Grill Grate. Close the hood, and GRILL for 8 minutes. After 8 minutes, flip the pork chops and baste the cooked side with the barbecue sauce. Close the hood, and GRILL for 5 minutes more.
5. Open the hood, and flip the pork chops again, basting both sides with the barbecue sauce. Close the hood, and GRILL for the final 2 minutes.
6. When cooking is complete, season with salt and pepper and serve immediately.

Golden Wasabi Spam

Servings: 3

Cooking Time: 12 Minutes

Ingredients:

- ⅔ cup all-purpose flour
- 2 large eggs
- 1½ tablespoons wasabi paste
- 2 cups panko breadcrumbs
- 6 ½-inch-thick spam slices
- Cooking spray

Directions:

1. Spritz the Crisper Basket with cooking spray.
2. Insert the Crisper Basket and close the hood. Select AIR CRISP, set the temperature to 400°F, and set the time to 12 minutes. Select START/STOP to begin preheating.
3. Pour the flour in a shallow plate. Whisk the eggs with wasabi in a large bowl. Pour the panko in a separate shallow plate.
4. Dredge the spam slices in the flour first, then dunk in the egg mixture, and then roll the spam over the panko to coat well. Shake the excess off.
5. Arrange the spam slices in a single layer in the basket and spritz with cooking spray.
6. Close the hood and AIR CRISP for 12 minutes or until the spam slices are golden and crispy. Flip the spam slices halfway through.
7. Serve immediately.

Potato And Prosciutto Salad

Servings: 8

Cooking Time: 7 Minutes

Ingredients:

- Salad:
- 4 pounds potatoes, boiled and cubed
- 15 slices prosciutto, diced
- 2 cups shredded Cheddar cheese
- Dressing:
- 15 ounces sour cream
- 2 tablespoons mayonnaise
- 1 teaspoon salt
- 1 teaspoon black pepper
- 1 teaspoon dried basil

Directions:

1. Select AIR CRISP, set the temperature to 350°F, and set the time to 7 minutes. Select START/STOP to begin preheating.
2. Put the potatoes, prosciutto, and Cheddar in a baking pan. Place the pan directly in the pot. Close the hood and AIR CRISP for 7 minutes.
3. In a separate bowl, mix the sour cream, mayonnaise, salt, pepper, and basil using a whisk.
4. Coat the salad with the dressing and serve.

Crackling Pork Roast

Servings: 8

Cooking Time: 1 Hour 30 Minutes

Ingredients:

- 1 (3- to 4-pound) boneless pork shoulder, rind on
- Kosher salt

Directions:

1. Pat the roast dry with a paper towel. Using a sharp knife, score the rind, creating a diamond pattern on top. Season generously with salt. Place it in the refrigerator, uncovered, overnight to brine.
2. Plug the thermometer into the unit. Insert the Cooking Pot and close the hood. Select ROAST, set the temperature to 350°F, then select PRESET. Use the arrows to the right to select PORK. The unit will default to WELL to cook pork to a safe temperature. Insert the Smart Thermometer into the thickest part of the meat. Select START/STOP to begin preheating.
3. When the unit beeps to signify it has preheated, place the roast in the Cooking Pot. Close the hood to begin cooking.
4. When cooking is complete, the Smart Thermometer will indicate that the desired temperature has been reached. Remove the pork and let it rest for 10 minutes before slicing.

Sauces, Dips, And Dressings

Sauces, Dips, And Dressings

Garlic Lime Tahini Dressing

Servings: 1

Cooking Time: 0 Minutes

Ingredients:

- ⅓ cup tahini
- 3 tablespoons filtered water
- 2 tablespoons freshly squeezed lime juice
- 1 tablespoon apple cider vinegar
- 1 teaspoon lime zest
- 1½ teaspoons raw honey
- ¼ teaspoon garlic powder
- ¼ teaspoon salt

Directions:

1. Whisk together the tahini, water, vinegar, lime juice, lime zest, honey, salt, and garlic powder in a small bowl until well emulsified.
2. Serve immediately, or refrigerate in an airtight container for to 1 week.

Ginger Sweet Sauce

Servings: 1

Cooking Time: 5 Minutes

Ingredients:

- 3 tablespoons ketchup
- 2 tablespoons water
- 2 tablespoons maple syrup
- 1 tablespoon rice vinegar
- 2 teaspoons peeled minced fresh ginger root
- 2 teaspoons soy sauce (or tamari, which is a gluten-free option)
- 1 teaspoon cornstarch

Directions:

1. In a small saucepan over medium heat, combine all the ingredients and stir continuously for 5 minutes, or until slightly thickened.
2. Enjoy warm or cold.

Lemon Dijon Vinaigrette

Servings: 6

Cooking Time: 0 Minutes

Ingredients:

- ¼ cup extra-virgin olive oil
- 1 garlic clove, minced
- 2 tablespoons freshly squeezed lemon juice
- 1 teaspoon Dijon mustard
- ½ teaspoon raw honey
- ¼ teaspoon salt
- ¼ teaspoon dried basil

Directions:

1. Place all the ingredients in a mason jar. Cover and shake vigorously until thoroughly mixed and well emulsified.
2. Serve chilled.

Creamy Ranch Dressing

Servings: 8

Cooking Time: 0 Minutes

Ingredients:

- 1 cup plain Greek yogurt
- ¼ cup chopped fresh dill
- 2 tablespoons chopped fresh chives
- Zest of 1 lemon
- 1 garlic clove, minced
- ½ teaspoon sea salt
- ⅛ teaspoon freshly cracked black pepper

Directions:

1. Mix together the yogurt, dill, chives, lemon zest, garlic, sea salt, and pepper in a small bowl and whisk to combine.
2. Serve chilled.

Pico De Gallo

Servings: 2

Cooking Time: 0 Minutes

Ingredients:

- 3 large tomatoes, chopped
- ½ small red onion, diced
- ⅛ cup chopped fresh cilantro
- 3 garlic cloves, chopped
- 2 tablespoons chopped pickled jalapeño pepper
- 1 tablespoon lime juice
- ¼ teaspoon pink Himalayan salt (optional)

Directions:

1. In a medium bowl, combine all the ingredients and mix with a wooden spoon.

Cashew Vodka Sauce

Servings: 3

Cooking Time: 5 Minutes

Ingredients:

- ¾ cup raw cashews
- ¼ cup boiling water
- 1 tablespoon olive oil
- 4 garlic cloves, minced
- 1½ cups unsweetened almond milk
- 1 tablespoon arrowroot powder
- 1 teaspoon salt
- 1 tablespoon nutritional yeast
- 1¼ cups marinara sauce

Directions:

1. Put the cashews in a heatproof bowl and add boiling water to cover. Let soak for 10 minutes. Drain the cashews and place them in a blender. Add ¼ cup boiling water and blend for 1 to 2 minutes or until creamy. Set aside.
2. In a small saucepan, heat the olive oil over medium heat. Add the garlic and sauté for 2 minutes until golden. Whisk in the almond milk, arrowroot powder, and salt. Bring to a simmer. Continue to simmer, whisking frequently, for about 5 minutes or until the sauce thickens.
3. Carefully transfer the hot almond milk mixture to the blender with the cashews. Blend for 30 seconds to combine, then add the nutritional yeast and marinara sauce. Blend for 1 minute or until creamy.

Balsamic Dressing

Servings: 1

Cooking Time: 0 Minutes

Ingredients:

- 2 tablespoons Dijon mustard
- ¼ cup balsamic vinegar
- ¾ cup olive oil

Directions:

1. Put all ingredients in a jar with a tight-fitting lid. Put on the lid and shake vigorously until thoroughly combined. Refrigerate until ready to use and shake well before serving.

Hummus

Servings: 2

Cooking Time: 0 Minutes

Ingredients:

- 1 can chickpeas, drained and rinsed
- ¼ cup tahini
- 3 tablespoons cold water
- 2 tablespoons freshly squeezed lemon juice
- 1 garlic clove
- ½ teaspoon turmeric powder
- ⅛ teaspoon black pepper
- Pinch of pink Himalayan salt

Directions:

1. Combine all the ingredients in a food processor and blend until smooth.

Cashew Pesto

Servings: 1

Cooking Time: 0 Minutes

Ingredients:

- ¼ cup raw cashews
- Juice of 1 lemon
- 2 garlic cloves
- ⅓ red onion
- 1 tablespoon olive oil
- 4 cups basil leaves, packed
- 1 cup wheatgrass
- ¼ cup water
- ¼ teaspoon salt

Directions:

1. Put the cashews in a heatproof bowl and add boiling water to cover. Soak for 5 minutes and then drain.
2. Put all ingredients in a blender and blend for 2 to 3 minutes or until fully combined.

Cashew Ranch Dressing

Servings: 12

Cooking Time: 0 Minutes

Ingredients:

- 1 cup cashews, soaked in warm water for at least 1 hour
- ½ cup water
- 2 tablespoons freshly squeezed lemon juice
- 1 tablespoon vinegar
- 1 teaspoon garlic powder
- 1 teaspoon onion powder
- 2 teaspoons dried dill

Directions:

1. In a food processor, combine the cashews, water, lemon juice, vinegar, garlic powder, and onion powder. Blend until creamy and smooth. Add the dill and pulse a few times until combined.

Poultry

Poultry

Lemon Parmesan Chicken

Servings: 4

Cooking Time: 20 Minutes

Ingredients:

- 1 egg
- 2 tablespoons lemon juice
- 2 teaspoons minced garlic
- ½ teaspoon salt
- ½ teaspoon freshly ground black pepper
- 4 boneless, skinless chicken breasts, thin cut
- Olive oil spray
- ½ cup whole-wheat bread crumbs
- ¼ cup grated Parmesan cheese

Directions:

1. In a medium bowl, whisk together the egg, lemon juice, garlic, salt, and pepper. Add the chicken breasts, cover, and refrigerate for up to 1 hour.
2. In a shallow bowl, combine the bread crumbs and Parmesan cheese.
3. Spray the Crisper Basket lightly with olive oil spray.
4. Insert the Crisper Basket and close the hood. Select AIR CRISP, set the temperature to 360°F, and set the time to 20 minutes. Select START/STOP to begin preheating.
5. Remove the chicken breasts from the egg mixture, then dredge them in the bread crumb mixture, and place in the Crisper Basket in a single layer. Lightly spray the chicken breasts with olive oil spray. You may need to cook the chicken in batches.
6. Close the hood and AIR CRISP for 8 minutes. Flip the chicken over, lightly spray with olive oil spray, and AIR CRISP for an additional 7 to 12 minutes, until the chicken reaches an internal temperature of 165°F.
7. Serve warm.

Pecan-crusted Turkey Cutlets

Servings: 4

Cooking Time: 10 To 12 Minutes

Ingredients:

- ¾ cup panko bread crumbs
- ¼ teaspoon salt
- ¼ teaspoon pepper
- ¼ teaspoon dry mustard
- ¼ teaspoon poultry seasoning
- ½ cup pecans
- ¼ cup cornstarch
- 1 egg, beaten
- 1 pound turkey cutlets, ½-inch thick
- Salt and pepper, to taste
- Cooking spray

Directions:

1. Insert the Crisper Basket and close the hood. Select AIR CRISP, set the temperature to 360°F, and set the time to 12 minutes. Select START/STOP to begin preheating.
2. Place the panko crumbs, salt, pepper, mustard, and poultry seasoning in a food processor. Process until crumbs are finely crushed. Add pecans and process just until nuts are finely chopped.
3. Place cornstarch in a shallow dish and beaten egg in another. Transfer coating mixture from food processor into a third shallow dish.
4. Sprinkle turkey cutlets with salt and pepper to taste.
5. Dip cutlets in cornstarch and shake off excess, then dip in beaten egg and finally roll in crumbs, pressing to coat well. Spray both sides with cooking spray.
6. Place 2 cutlets in Crisper Basket in a single layer. Close the hood and AIR CRISP for 10 to 12 minutes. Repeat with the remaining cutlets.
7. Serve warm.

Salsa Verde Chicken Enchiladas

Servings: 4

Cooking Time: 20 Minutes

Ingredients:

- 1 tablespoon chili powder
- 1 teaspoon onion powder
- 1 teaspoon garlic powder
- 1 teaspoon ground cumin
- 2 teaspoons salt
- 3 boneless, skinless chicken breasts (about 1½ pounds)
- Extra-virgin olive oil
- 1 (16-ounce) jar salsa verde
- 2 cups shredded Mexican-style cheese blend
- 6 (8-inch) flour tortillas
- Diced tomatoes, for topping
- Sour cream, for topping

Directions:

1. Insert the Grill Grate and close the hood. Select GRILL, set the temperature to MED, and set the time to 12 minutes. Select START/STOP to begin preheating.
2. While the unit is preheating, in a small bowl, combine the chili powder, onion powder, garlic powder, ground cumin, and salt. Drizzle the chicken breasts with the olive oil and season the meat on both sides with the seasoning mixture.
3. When the unit beeps to signify it has preheated, place the chicken breasts on the Grill Grate. Close the hood and cook for 6 minutes.
4. After 6 minutes, open the hood and flip the chicken. Close the hood and cook for 6 minutes more.
5. When cooking is complete, open the hood and use grill mitts to remove the Grill Grate and chicken breasts. Let the chicken breasts cool for about 5 minutes. Use two forks to shred the chicken, or cut it into small chunks.
6. To assemble the enchiladas, place a generous amount of chicken on a tortilla. Lift one end of the tortilla and roll it over and around the chicken. Do not fold in the sides of the tortilla as you roll. Place the enchilada, seam-side down, in the Cooking Pot. Repeat with the remaining 5 tortillas and the rest of the chicken. Pour the salsa verde over the enchiladas, completely covering them. Top the salsa with the shredded cheese.
7. Select BAKE, set the temperature to 350°F, and set the time to 8 minutes. Select START/STOP and then press the PREHEAT button to skip preheating. Close the hood and cook for 8 minutes.
8. When cooking is complete, remove the enchiladas from the pot and serve topped with the diced tomatoes and sour cream.

Grilled Turkey Pesto Sandwiches

Servings: 4

Cooking Time: 6 Minutes

Ingredients:

- 4 tablespoons (½ stick) unsalted butter, at room temperature
- 8 slices sourdough bread
- 4 tablespoons jarred pesto
- 1 (16-ounce) package deli turkey meat (4 slices per sandwich)
- 4 slices Monterey Jack cheese

Directions:

1. Insert the Grill Grate and close the hood. Select GRILL, set the temperature to LO, and set the time to 6 minutes. Select START/STOP to begin preheating.
2. While the unit is preheating, spread about ½ tablespoon of butter on the outside of each bread slice. Flip the slices over so the buttered sides are down. Spread about ½ tablespoon of pesto on the unbuttered side of each slice. Place 4 slices of turkey and 1 slice of cheese on top of the pesto on half of the bread slices. Close each sandwich with the other 4 slices, butter-side up.
3. When the unit beeps to signify it has preheated, place the sandwiches on the Grill Grate. Close the hood and cook for 3 minutes.
4. After 3 minutes, open the hood and flip the sandwiches. Close the hood and cook for 3 minutes more.
5. When cooking is complete, the bread will be lightly browned and toasted and the cheese will be melted. Remove from the grill and serve.

Buttermilk Ranch Chicken Tenders

Servings: 4

Cooking Time: 10 Minutes

Ingredients:

- 2 cups buttermilk
- 1 (0.4-ounce) packet ranch seasoning mix
- 1½ pounds boneless, skinless chicken breasts (about 3 breasts), cut into 1-inch strips
- 2 cups all-purpose flour
- ¼ teaspoon paprika
- ¼ teaspoon garlic powder
- ¼ teaspoon baking powder
- 2 teaspoons salt
- 2 large eggs
- ¼ cup avocado oil, divided

Directions:

1. In a large bowl, whisk together the buttermilk and ranch seasoning. Place the chicken strips in the bowl. Cover and let marinate in the refrigerator for 30 minutes.
2. Create an assembly line with 2 large bowls. Combine the flour, paprika, garlic powder, baking powder, and salt in one bowl. In the other bowl, whisk together the eggs. One at a time, remove the chicken strips from the marinade, shaking off any excess liquid. Dredge the chicken strip in the seasoned flour, coating both sides, then dip it in the beaten egg. Finally, dip it back into the seasoned flour bowl again. Shake any excess flour off. Repeat the process with all the chicken strips, setting them aside on a flat tray or plate once coated.
3. Insert the Grill Grate and close the hood. Select GRILL, set the temperature to MED, and set the time to 10 minutes. Select START/STOP to begin preheating.
4. While the unit is preheating, use a basting brush to generously coat one side of the chicken strips with half of the avocado oil.
5. When the unit beeps to signify it has preheated, place the chicken strips on the grill, oiled-side down. Brush the top of the chicken strips with the rest of the avocado oil. Close the hood and grill for 5 minutes.
6. After 5 minutes, open the hood and flip the chicken strips. Close the hood and continue cooking for 5 minutes more.
7. When cooking is complete, the chicken strips will be golden brown and crispy. Remove them from the grill and serve.

Sweet Chili Turkey Kebabs

Servings: 4

Cooking Time: 12 Minutes

Ingredients:

- 2 pounds turkey breast, cut into 1-inch cubes
- ¼ cup honey
- 1 tablespoon extra-virgin olive oil
- 2 tablespoons apple cider vinegar
- 2 tablespoons soy sauce
- Juice of 1 lime
- 1 teaspoon red pepper flakes

Directions:

1. Place 5 or 6 turkey cubes on each of 8 to 10 skewers. In a zip-top bag, combine the honey, olive oil, vinegar, soy sauce, lime juice, and red pepper flakes. Shake to mix well. Place the turkey skewers in the marinade and massage to coat the meat. Seal the bag and let marinate at room temperature for 30 minutes or in the refrigerator overnight.
2. Insert the Grill Grate and close the hood. Select GRILL, set the temperature to MED, and set the time to 12 minutes. Select START/STOP to begin preheating.
3. When the unit beeps to signify it has preheated, place half of the skewers on the Grill Grate. Brush extra glaze on the skewers. Close the hood and grill for 3 minutes.
4. After 3 minutes, open the hood and flip the skewers. Close the hood and cook for 3 minutes more.
5. After 3 minutes, remove the skewers from the grill. Repeat steps 3 and 4 for the remaining skewers.
6. When cooking is complete, remove the kebabs from the grill and serve.

BBQ Grill & Smoker Cookbook

Chicken Cordon Bleu Roll-ups

Servings: 4

Cooking Time: 15 Minutes

Ingredients:

- 1 tablespoon garlic powder
- 1 tablespoon onion powder
- 1½ pounds boneless, skinless chicken breasts (about 3 breasts)
- 6 ounces thin-sliced deli ham
- 6 ounces Swiss cheese, sliced
- 2 large eggs
- 1 cup plain bread crumbs
- ¼ cup sour cream
- 3 tablespoons Dijon mustard
- ¼ teaspoon granulated sugar or honey

Directions:

1. Insert the Grill Grate and close the hood. Select GRILL, set the temperature to MED, and set the time to 15 minutes. Select START/STOP to begin preheating.
2. In a small bowl, combine the garlic powder and onion powder.
3. Cut each chicken breast in half from the side (parallel to the cutting board) to create 6 thinner, flatter chicken breasts. Lightly coat the chicken all over with the garlic-and-onion mixture.
4. Layer 3 or 4 slices of ham on top of each piece of chicken, and top with about 1 ounce of cheese. Starting at the short end, roll the chicken breasts to wrap the ham and cheese inside. Secure the chicken roll-ups with toothpicks.
5. In a large bowl, whisk the eggs. Put the bread crumbs in a separate large bowl. Dip the chicken roll-ups in the egg and then into the bread crumbs until fully coated.
6. When the unit beeps to signify it has preheated, place the roll-ups on the Grill Grate. Close the hood and grill for 7 minutes, 30 seconds.
7. After 7 minutes, 30 seconds, open the hood and flip the roll-ups. Close the hood and continue cooking for 7 minutes, 30 seconds more.
8. While the roll-ups are cooking, in a small bowl, combine the sour cream, Dijon mustard, and sugar and stir until the sugar is dissolved.
9. When cooking is complete, remove the roll-ups from the grill and serve with the sauce, for dipping.

Ginger Chicken Thighs

Servings: 4

Cooking Time: 10 Minutes

Ingredients:

- ¼ cup julienned peeled fresh ginger
- 2 tablespoons vegetable oil
- 1 tablespoon honey
- 1 tablespoon soy sauce
- 1 tablespoon ketchup
- 1 teaspoon garam masala
- 1 teaspoon ground turmeric
- ¼ teaspoon kosher salt
- ½ teaspoon cayenne pepper
- Vegetable oil spray
- 1 pound boneless, skinless chicken thighs, cut crosswise into thirds
- ¼ cup chopped fresh cilantro, for garnish

Directions:

1. In a small bowl, combine the ginger, oil, honey, soy sauce, ketchup, garam masala, turmeric, salt, and cayenne. Whisk until well combined. Place the chicken in a resealable plastic bag and pour the marinade over. Seal the bag and massage to cover all of the chicken with the marinade. Marinate at room temperature for 30 minutes or in the refrigerator for up to 24 hours.
2. Insert the Crisper Basket and close the hood. Select BAKE, set the temperature to 350ºF, and set the time to 10 minutes. Select START/STOP to begin preheating.
3. Spray the Crisper Basket with vegetable oil spray and add the chicken and as much of the marinade and julienned ginger as possible.
4. Close the hood and BAKE for 10 minutes. Use a meat thermometer to ensure the chicken has reached an internal temperature of 165ºF.
5. To serve, garnish with cilantro.

Deep Fried Duck Leg Quarters

Servings: 4

Cooking Time: 45 Minutes

Ingredients:

- 4 skin-on duck leg quarters
- 2 medium garlic cloves, minced
- ½ teaspoon salt
- ½ teaspoon ground black pepper

Directions:

1. Spritz the Crisper Basket with cooking spray.
2. Insert the Crisper Basket and close the hood. Select AIR CRISP, set the temperature to 300ºF, and set the time to 45 minutes. Select START/STOP to begin preheating.
3. On a clean work surface, rub the duck leg quarters with garlic, salt, and black pepper.
4. Arrange the leg quarters in the basket and spritz with cooking spray.
5. Close the hood and AIR CRISP for 30 minutes, then flip the leg quarters and increase the temperature to 375ºF. AIR CRISP for 15 more minutes or until well browned and crispy.
6. Remove the duck leg quarters from the grill and allow to cool for 10 minutes before serving.

Simple Whole Chicken Bake

Servings: 2 To 4

Cooking Time: 1 Hour

Ingredients:

- ½ cup melted butter
- 3 tablespoons garlic, minced
- Salt, to taste
- 1 teaspoon ground black pepper
- 1 whole chicken

Directions:

1. Select BAKE, set the temperature to 350ºF, and set the time to 1 hour. Select START/STOP to begin preheating.
2. Combine the butter with garlic, salt, and ground black pepper in a small bowl.
3. Brush the butter mixture over the whole chicken, then place the chicken in a baking pan, skin side down.
4. Place the pan directly in the pot. Close the hood and BAKE for 1 hour, or until an instant-read thermometer inserted in the thickest part of the chicken registers at least 165ºF. Flip the chicken halfway through.
5. Remove the chicken from the grill and allow to cool for 15 minutes before serving.

Teriyaki Chicken And Bell Pepper Kebabs

Servings: 4

Cooking Time: 14 Minutes

Ingredients:

- 1 pound boneless, skinless chicken breasts, cut into 2-inch cubes
- 1 cup teriyaki sauce, divided
- 2 green bell peppers, seeded and cut into 1-inch cubes
- 2 cups fresh pineapple, cut into 1-inch cubes

Directions:

1. Place the chicken and ½ cup of teriyaki sauce in a large resealable plastic bag or container. Toss to coat evenly. Refrigerate for at least 30 minutes.
2. Insert the Grill Grate and close the hood. Select GRILL, set the temperature to MEDIUM, and set the time to 14 minutes. Select START/STOP to begin preheating.
3. While the unit is preheating, assemble the kebabs by threading the chicken onto the wood skewers, alternating with the peppers and pineapple. Ensure the ingredients are pushed almost completely down to the end of the skewers.
4. When the unit beeps to signify it has preheated, place the skewers on the Grill Grate. Close the hood and GRILL for 10 to 14 minutes, occasionally basting the kebabs with the remaining ½ cup of teriyaki sauce while cooking.
5. Cooking is complete when the internal temperature of the chicken reaches 165ºF on a food thermometer.

Turkey Meatballs With Cranberry Sauce

Servings: 4

Cooking Time: 20 Minutes

Ingredients:

- 2 tablespoons onion powder
- 1 cup plain bread crumbs
- 2 large eggs
- 2 tablespoons light brown sugar, packed
- 1 tablespoon salt
- 2 pounds ground turkey
- 1 (14-ounce) can cranberry sauce

Directions:

1. In a large bowl, mix together the onion powder, bread crumbs, eggs, brown sugar, and salt. Place the ground turkey in the bowl. Using your hands, mix the ingredients together just until combined (overmixing can make the meat tough and chewy). Form the mixture into 1½- to 2-inch meatballs. This should make 20 to 22 meatballs.
2. Insert the Grill Grate and close the hood. Select GRILL, set the temperature to MED, and set the time to 20 minutes. Select START/STOP to begin preheating.
3. When the unit beeps to signify it has preheated, place the meatballs on the Grill Grate. Close the hood and cook for 10 minutes.
4. After 10 minutes, open the hood and flip the meatballs. Close the hood and cook for 10 minutes more.
5. When cooking is complete, remove the meatballs from the grill. Place the cranberry sauce in a small bowl and use a whisk to stir it into more of a thick jelly sauce. Serve the meatballs with the sauce on the side.

Adobo Chicken

Servings: 4

Cooking Time: 15 Minutes

Ingredients:

- 2 tablespoons soy sauce
- 2 tablespoons rice vinegar
- 1 tablespoon balsamic vinegar
- ¼ teaspoon freshly ground black pepper
- 4 garlic cloves, minced
- ½ teaspoon peeled minced fresh ginger
- Juice of ½ lemon
- ¼ teaspoon granulated sugar
- 3 bay leaves
- Pinch Italian seasoning (optional)
- Pinch ground cumin (optional)
- 3 pounds chicken drumsticks

Directions:

1. In a large bowl, whisk together the soy sauce, rice vinegar, balsamic vinegar, pepper, garlic, ginger, lemon juice, sugar, bay leaves, Italian seasoning (if using), and cumin (if using). Add the drumsticks to the marinade, making sure the meat is coated. Cover and refrigerate for at least 1 hour. If you have the time, marinate the chicken overnight to let all the flavors settle in.
2. Insert the Grill Grate and close the hood. Select GRILL, set the temperature to MED, and set the time to 15 minutes. Select START/STOP to begin preheating.
3. When the unit beeps to signify it has preheated, place the chicken drumsticks on the Grill Grate. Brush any leftover marinade onto the drumsticks. Close the hood and grill for 8 minutes.
4. After 8 minutes, open the hood and flip the drumsticks. Close the hood and continue cooking for 7 minutes more.
5. When cooking is complete, remove the drumsticks from the grill and serve.

Spicy Chicken Kebabs

Servings: 4

Cooking Time: 14 Minutes

Ingredients:

- 1 tablespoon ground cumin
- 1 tablespoon garlic powder
- 1 tablespoon chili powder
- 2 teaspoons paprika
- ¼ teaspoon sea salt
- ¼ teaspoon freshly ground black pepper
- 1 pound boneless, skinless chicken breasts, cut in 2-inch cubes
- 2 tablespoons extra-virgin olive oil, divided
- 2 red bell peppers, seeded and cut into 1-inch cubes
- 1 red onion, quartered
- Juice of 1 lime

Directions:

1. In a small mixing bowl, combine the cumin, garlic powder, chili powder, paprika, salt, and pepper, and mix well.
2. Place the chicken, 1 tablespoon oil, and half of the spice mixture into a large resealable plastic bag or container. Toss to coat evenly.
3. Place the bell pepper, onion, remaining 1 tablespoon of oil, and remaining spice mixture into a large resealable plastic bag or container. Toss to coat evenly. Refrigerate the chicken and vegetables for at least 30 minutes.
4. Insert the Grill Grate and close the hood. Select GRILL, set the temperature to HIGH, and set the time to 14 minutes. Select START/STOP to begin preheating.
5. While the unit is preheating, assemble the kebabs by threading the chicken onto the wood skewers, alternating with the peppers and onion. Ensure the ingredients are pushed almost completely down to the end of the skewers.
6. When the unit beeps to signify it has preheated, place the skewers on the Grill Grate. Close the hood and GRILL for 10 to 14 minutes.
7. Cooking is complete when the internal temperature of the chicken reaches 165°F. When cooking is complete, remove from the heat, and drizzle with lime juice.

Lettuce Chicken Tacos With Peanut Sauce

Servings: 4

Cooking Time: 6 Minutes

Ingredients:

- 1 pound ground chicken
- 2 cloves garlic, minced
- ¼ cup diced onions
- ¼ teaspoon sea salt
- Cooking spray
- Peanut Sauce:
- ¼ cup creamy peanut butter, at room temperature
- 2 tablespoons tamari
- 1½ teaspoons hot sauce
- 2 tablespoons lime juice
- 2 tablespoons grated fresh ginger
- 2 tablespoons chicken broth
- 2 teaspoons sugar
- For Serving:
- 2 small heads butter lettuce, leaves separated
- Lime slices (optional)

Directions:

1. Select BAKE, set the temperature to 350°F, and set the time to 5 minutes. Select START/STOP to begin preheating.
2. Spritz a baking pan with cooking spray.
3. Combine the ground chicken, garlic, and onions in the baking pan, then sprinkle with salt. Use a fork to break the ground chicken and combine them well.
4. Place the pan directly in the pot. Close the hood and BAKE for 5 minutes, or until the chicken is lightly browned. Stir them halfway through the cooking time.
5. Meanwhile, combine the ingredients for the sauce in a small bowl. Stir to mix well.
6. Pour the sauce in the pan of chicken, then cook for 1 more minute or until heated through.
7. Unfold the lettuce leaves on a large serving plate, then divide the chicken mixture on the lettuce leaves. Drizzle with lime juice and serve immediately.

Rosemary Turkey Breast

Servings: 6

Cooking Time: 30 Minutes

Ingredients:

- ½ teaspoon dried rosemary
- 2 minced garlic cloves
- 2 teaspoons salt
- 1 teaspoon ground black pepper
- ¼ cup olive oil
- 2½ pounds turkey breast
- ¼ cup pure maple syrup
- 1 tablespoon stone-ground brown mustard
- 1 tablespoon melted vegan butter

Directions:

1. Combine the rosemary, garlic, salt, ground black pepper, and olive oil in a large bowl. Stir to mix well.
2. Dunk the turkey breast in the mixture and wrap the bowl in plastic. Refrigerate for 2 hours to marinate.
3. Remove the bowl from the refrigerator and let sit for half an hour before cooking.
4. Spritz the Crisper Basket with cooking spray.
5. Insert the Crisper Basket and close the hood. Select AIR CRISP, set the temperature to 400°F, and set the time to 30 minutes. Select START/STOP to begin preheating.
6. Remove the turkey from the marinade and place in the basket. Close the hood and AIR CRISP for 20 minutes or until well browned. Flip the breast halfway through.
7. Meanwhile, combine the remaining ingredients in a small bowl. Stir to mix well.
8. Pour half of the butter mixture over the turkey breast in the basket. Close the hood and AIR CRISP for 10 more minutes. Flip the breast and pour the remaining half of butter mixture over halfway through.
9. Transfer the turkey on a plate and slice to serve.

Lime-garlic Grilled Chicken

Servings: 4

Cooking Time: 18 Minutes

Ingredients:

- 1½ tablespoons extra-virgin olive oil
- 3 garlic cloves, minced
- ¼ teaspoon ground cumin
- Sea salt, to taste
- Freshly ground black pepper, to taste
- Grated zest of 1 lime
- Juice of 1 lime
- 4 boneless, skinless chicken breasts

Directions:

1. In a large shallow bowl, stir together the oil, garlic, cumin, salt, pepper, zest, and lime juice. Add the chicken breasts and coat well. Cover and marinate in the refrigerator for 30 minutes.
2. Insert the Grill Grate and close the hood. Select GRILL, set the temperature to MEDIUM, and set the time to 18 minutes. Select START/STOP to begin preheating.
3. When the unit has beeped to signify it has preheated, place the chicken breasts on the Grill Grate. Close the hood and GRILL for 7 minutes. After 7 minutes, flip the chicken, close the hood, and GRILL for an additional 7 minutes.
4. Check the chicken for doneness. If needed, GRILL up to 4 minutes more. Cooking is complete when the internal temperature of the chicken reaches at least 165°F on a food thermometer.
5. Remove from the grill, and place on a cutting board or platter to rest for 5inutes. Serve.

Grilled Cornish Hens

Servings: 4

Cooking Time: 20 Minutes

Ingredients:

- ½ cup avocado oil
- 1 teaspoon dried oregano
- ½ teaspoon freshly ground black pepper
- 1 teaspoon garlic salt
- 2 tablespoons minced garlic
- 1 teaspoon chopped fresh thyme
- 1 teaspoon chopped fresh parsley
- 1 teaspoon chopped fresh rosemary
- 2 (1-pound) Cornish hens
- 1 large yellow onion, halved
- 4 garlic cloves, peeled

Directions:

1. Plug the thermometer into the unit. Insert the Grill Grate and close the hood. Select GRILL, set the temperature to LO, then select PRESET. Use the arrows to the right to select CHICKEN. The unit will default to WELL to cook poultry to a safe temperature. Select START/STOP to begin preheating.
2. While the unit is preheating, place the Smart Thermometer into the thickest part of the breast of one of the hens. In a small bowl, whisk together the avocado oil, oregano, pepper, garlic salt, minced garlic, thyme, parsley, and rosemary. Cut a few small slits in the skin of each Cornish hen. Rub the seasoning oil all over the skin and between the skin and meat where you made the slits. Place an onion half and 2 garlic cloves inside the cavity of each hen.
3. When the unit beeps to signify it has preheated, place the hens on the Grill Grate. Close the hood and cook.
4. When the Foodi™ Grill tells you, open the hood and flip the hens. Close the hood and continue to cook.
5. When cooking is complete, remove the hens from the grill and let sit for 5 minutes. Serve.

Crispy Dill Pickle Chicken Wings

Servings: 4

Cooking Time: 26 Minutes

Ingredients:

- 2 pounds bone-in chicken wings (drumettes and flats)
- 1½ cups dill pickle juice
- 1½ tablespoons vegetable oil
- ½ tablespoon dried dill
- ¾ teaspoon garlic powder
- Sea salt, to taste
- Freshly ground black pepper, to taste

Directions:

1. Place the chicken wings in a large shallow bowl. Pour the pickle juice over the top, ensuring all of the wings are coated and as submerged as possible. Cover and refrigerate for 2 hours.
2. Insert the Crisper Basket and close the hood. Select AIR CRISP, set the temperature to 390°F, and set the time to 26 minutes. Select START/STOP to begin preheating.
3. While the unit is preheating, rinse the brined chicken wings under cool water, then pat them dry with a paper towel. Place in a large bowl.
4. In a small bowl, whisk together the oil, dill, garlic powder, salt, and pepper. Drizzle over the wings and toss to fully coat them.
5. When the unit beeps to signify it has preheated, place the wings in the basket, spreading them out evenly. Close the hood and AIR CRISP for 11 minutes.
6. After 11 minutes, flip the wings with tongs. Close the hood and AIR CRISP for 11 minutes more.
7. Check the wings for doneness. Cooking is complete when the internal temperature of the chicken reaches at least 165°F on a food thermometer. If needed, AIR CRISP for up to 4 more minutes.
8. Remove the wings from the basket and serve immediately.

Lemony Chicken And Veggie Kebabs

Servings: 4

Cooking Time: 14 Minutes

Ingredients:

- 2 tablespoons plain Greek yogurt
- ¼ cup extra-virgin olive oil
- Juice of 4 lemons
- Grated zest of 1 lemon
- 4 garlic cloves, minced
- 2 tablespoons dried oregano
- 1 teaspoon sea salt
- ½ teaspoon freshly ground black pepper
- 1 pound boneless, skinless chicken breasts, cut into 2-inch cubes
- 1 red onion, quartered
- 1 zucchini, sliced

Directions:

1. In a large bowl, whisk together the Greek yogurt, oil, lemon juice, zest, garlic, oregano, salt, and pepper until well combined.
2. Place the chicken and half of the marinade into a large resealable plastic bag or container. Move the chicken around to coat evenly. Refrigerate for at least 30 minutes.
3. Insert the Grill Grate and close the hood. Select GRILL, set the temperature to MEDIUM, and set the time to 14 minutes. Select START/STOP to begin preheating.
4. While the unit is preheating, assemble the kebabs by threading the chicken on the wood skewers, alternating with the red onion and zucchini. Ensure the ingredients are pushed almost completely down to the end of the skewers.
5. When the unit beeps to signify it has preheated, place the skewers on the Grill Grate. Close hood and GRILL for 10 to 14 minutes, occasionally basting the kebabs with the remaining marinade while cooking.
6. Cooking is complete when the internal temperature of the chicken reaches 165°F on a food thermometer.

Garlic Brown-butter Chicken With Tomatoes

Servings: 4

Cooking Time: 15 Minutes

Ingredients:

- 4 boneless, skinless chicken breasts
- Extra-virgin olive oil
- ½ teaspoon paprika
- ½ teaspoon sea salt
- 12 tablespoons (1½ sticks) unsalted butter
- 4 garlic cloves, minced
- 2 tablespoons light brown sugar, packed
- ½ teaspoon garlic powder
- 6 ounces cherry tomatoes

Directions:

1. Insert the Cooking Pot and close the hood. Select GRILL, set the temperature to MED, and set the time to 15 minutes. Select START/STOP to begin preheating.
2. While the unit is preheating, drizzle the chicken breasts with olive oil, then lightly sprinkle both sides with the paprika and salt.
3. When the unit beeps to signify it has preheated, place the butter and garlic in the Cooking Pot. Insert the Grill Grate on top and place the chicken breasts on the Grill Grate. Close the hood and grill for 8 minutes.
4. After 8 minutes, open the hood and use grill mitts to remove the Grill Grate and chicken. Add the brown sugar, garlic powder, and tomatoes to the butter and garlic and stir.
5. Transfer the chicken to the Cooking Pot, making sure you flip the breasts. Coat the chicken with the brown butter sauce. Close the hood and cook for 7 minutes more.
6. When cooking is complete, remove the chicken and place on a plate. Spoon the sauce over and serve.

Crispy Chicken Strips

Servings: 4

Cooking Time: 20 Minutes

Ingredients:

- 1 tablespoon olive oil
- 1 pound boneless, skinless chicken tenderloins
- 1 teaspoon salt
- ½ teaspoon freshly ground black pepper
- ½ teaspoon paprika
- ½ teaspoon garlic powder
- ½ cup whole-wheat seasoned bread crumbs
- 1 teaspoon dried parsley
- Cooking spray

Directions:

1. Spray the Crisper Basket lightly with cooking spray.
2. Insert the Crisper Basket and close the hood. Select AIR CRISP, set the temperature to 370°F, and set the time to 20 minutes. Select START/STOP to begin preheating.
3. In a medium bowl, toss the chicken with the salt, pepper, paprika, and garlic powder until evenly coated.
4. Add the olive oil and toss to coat the chicken evenly.
5. In a separate, shallow bowl, mix together the bread crumbs and parsley.
6. Coat each piece of chicken evenly in the bread crumb mixture.
7. Place the chicken in the Crisper Basket in a single layer and spray it lightly with cooking spray. You may need to cook them in batches.
8. Close the hood and AIR CRISP for 10 minutes. Flip the chicken over, lightly spray it with cooking spray, and AIR CRISP for an additional 8 to 10 minutes, until golden brown. Serve.

Crispy Chicken Parmigiana

Servings: 4

Cooking Time: 15 Minutes

Ingredients:

- 2 large eggs
- 2 cups panko bread crumbs
- ½ cup shredded Parmesan cheese
- 1 tablespoon Italian seasoning
- 1 teaspoon garlic powder
- 1½ pounds boneless, skinless chicken breasts (about 3 breasts), halved lengthwise
- 3 cups marinara sauce, hot
- ½ cup grated Parmesan cheese

Directions:

1. Insert the Grill Grate and close the hood. Select GRILL, set the temperature to MED, and set the time to 15 minutes. Select START/STOP to begin preheating.
2. While the unit is preheating, create an assembly line with 2 large bowls. In one bowl, whisk the eggs. In the other bowl, combine the panko bread crumbs, shredded Parmesan cheese, Italian seasoning, and garlic powder. Dip each chicken breast in the egg and then into the bread crumb mix until fully coated. Set the coated chicken on a plate or tray.
3. When the unit beeps to signify it has preheated, place the chicken on the Grill Grate. Close the hood and grill for 8 minutes.
4. After 8 minutes, open the hood and flip the chicken. Close the hood and continue cooking for 7 minutes more.
5. When cooking is complete, remove the chicken from the grill and top with the marinara sauce and grated Parmesan cheese.

Seafood

Seafood

Chili-lime Shrimp Skewers

Servings: 4

Cooking Time: 10 Minutes

Ingredients:

- 2 pounds jumbo shrimp, peeled
- 1 tablespoon chili powder
- ¼ teaspoon ground cumin
- ¼ teaspoon dried oregano
- ¼ teaspoon garlic powder
- 2 tablespoons honey
- Juice of 2 limes, divided
- Instant rice, prepared as directed

Directions:

1. Insert the Grill Grate and close the hood. Select GRILL, set the temperature to HI, and set the time to 5 minutes. Select START/STOP to begin preheating.
2. While the unit is preheating, thread 4 or 5 shrimp onto each of 8 skewers, leaving about an inch of space at the bottom. Place the skewers on a large plate.
3. In a small bowl, combine the chili powder, cumin, oregano, and garlic powder. Lightly coat the shrimp with the dry rub. In the same bowl, add the honey and the juice of ½ lime to any remaining seasoning. Mix together.
4. When the unit beeps to signify it has preheated, place 4 shrimp skewers on the Grill Grate. Brush the shrimp with some of the honey mixture. Close the hood and grill for 2 minutes, 30 seconds.
5. After 2 minutes, 30 seconds, open the hood and squeeze the juice of another ½ lime over the skewers and flip. Brush on more honey mixture. Close the hood and cook for 2 minutes, 30 seconds.
6. When cooking is complete, the shrimp should be opaque and pink. Remove the skewers from the grill. Select GRILL, set the temperature to HI, and set the time to 5 minutes. Select START/STOP to begin and press PREHEAT to skip preheating. Repeat steps 4 and 5 for the remaining 4 skewers. When all of the skewers are cooked, serve with the rice.

Shrimp Boil

Servings: 6

Cooking Time: 10 Minutes

Ingredients:

- 2 tablespoons lemon-pepper seasoning
- 2 tablespoons light brown sugar, packed
- 2 tablespoons minced garlic
- 2 tablespoons Old Bay seasoning
- ¼ teaspoon Cajun seasoning
- ¼ teaspoon paprika
- ¼ teaspoon cayenne pepper
- 1 teaspoon garlic powder
- 1½ cups (3 sticks) unsalted butter, cut into quarters
- 2 pounds shrimp

Directions:

1. Insert the Cooking Pot and close the hood. Select GRILL, set the temperature to MED, and set the time to 10 minutes. Select START/STOP to begin preheating.
2. While the unit is preheating, in a small bowl, combine the lemon pepper, brown sugar, minced garlic, Old Bay seasoning, Cajun seasoning, paprika, cayenne pepper, and garlic powder.
3. When the unit beeps to signify it has preheated, place the butter and the lemon-pepper mixture in the Cooking Pot. Insert the Grill Grate and place the shrimp on it in a single layer. Close the hood and grill for 5 minutes.
4. After 5 minutes, open the hood and use grill mitts to remove the Grill Grate. Place the shrimp in the Cooking Pot. Stir to combine. Close the hood and cook for 5 minutes more.
5. When cooking is complete, open the hood and stir once more. Then close the hood and let the butter set with the shrimp for 5 minutes. Serve.

Grilled Mahi-mahi Tacos With Spicy Coleslaw

Servings: 4

Cooking Time: 10 Minutes

Ingredients:

- 1 teaspoon garlic powder
- 1 teaspoon onion powder
- 1 tablespoon paprika
- ¼ teaspoon salt
- 4 (8-ounce) mahi-mahi fillets
- Avocado oil
- Juice of 2 limes, divided
- 1 cup mayonnaise
- 1 tablespoon sriracha
- ⅛ teaspoon cayenne pepper
- ½ head red cabbage, shredded
- 8 (6-inch) corn tortillas

Directions:

1. Insert the Grill Grate and close the hood. Select GRILL, set the temperature to MED, and set the time to 10 minutes. Select START/STOP to begin preheating.
2. While the unit is preheating, in a small bowl, combine the garlic powder, onion powder, paprika, and salt. Place the mahi-mahi fillets on a large plate and rub avocado oil on both sides. Then squeeze the juice of 1 lime on top and generously coat the fillets with the seasoning mix.
3. When the unit beeps to signify it has preheated, place the fillets on the Grill Grate. Close the hood and grill for 8 minutes.
4. While the mahi-mahi is cooking, in a large bowl, combine the mayonnaise, sriracha, cayenne pepper, and the juice of the remaining lime. Add the shredded cabbage to the bowl and stir until combined.
5. After 8 minutes, open the hood and remove the fillets from the grill. Place the tortillas on the Grill Grate. Close the hood to warm them for 2 minutes. Feel free to flip after 1 minute, if desired.
6. Cut the mahi-mahi into ½-inch to 1-inch strips. To assemble the tacos, place the mahi-mahi pieces on the tortillas and dress with the spicy coleslaw mix. Serve.

Honey-walnut Shrimp

Servings: 4

Cooking Time: 8 Minutes

Ingredients:

- 2 ounces walnuts
- 2 tablespoons honey
- 1 egg
- 1 cup panko bread crumbs
- 1 pound shrimp, peeled
- ½ cup mayonnaise
- 1 teaspoon powdered sugar
- 2 tablespoons heavy (whipping) cream
- Scallions, both white and green parts, sliced, for garnish

Directions:

1. Insert the Grill Grate. In a small heat-safe bowl, combine the walnuts and honey, then place the bowl on the Grill Grate and close the hood. Select GRILL, set the temperature to HI, and set the time to 8 minutes. Select START/STOP to begin preheating. After 2 minutes of preheating (set a separate timer), remove the bowl. Close the hood to continue preheating.
2. While the unit is preheating, create an assembly line with 2 large bowls. In the first bowl, whisk the egg. Put the panko bread crumbs in the other bowl. One at a time, dip the shrimp in the egg and then into the panko bread crumbs until well coated. Place the breaded shrimp on a plate.
3. When the unit beeps to signify it has preheated, place the shrimp on the Grill Grate in a single layer. Close the hood and cook for 4 minutes.
4. After 4 minutes, open the hood and flip the shrimp. Close the hood and cook for 4 minutes more.
5. While the shrimp are cooking, in a large bowl, combine the mayonnaise, powdered sugar, and heavy cream and mix until the sugar has dissolved.
6. When cooking is complete, remove the shrimp from the grill. Add the cooked shrimp and honey walnuts to the mayonnaise mixture and gently fold them together. Garnish with scallions and serve.

BBQ Grill & Smoker Cookbook

Crab Cakes With Lemon-garlic Aioli

Servings: 12

Cooking Time: 16 Minutes

Ingredients:

- For the crab cakes
- 1 large egg
- 1 tablespoon Old Bay seasoning
- 1 tablespoon dried parsley
- 1 tablespoon soy sauce
- 1 tablespoon minced garlic
- ¼ cup grated Parmesan cheese
- ½ cup mayonnaise
- ½ cup panko bread crumbs
- 1 pound lump crabmeat
- Avocado oil cooking spray
- For the lemon-garlic aioli
- ½ cup mayonnaise
- 1 teaspoon garlic powder
- Juice of 1 lemon
- ¼ teaspoon paprika

Directions:

1. In a large bowl, whisk the egg, then add the Old Bay seasoning, parsley, soy sauce, garlic, Parmesan cheese, mayonnaise, and panko bread crumbs and mix well. Add the crabmeat and fold it in gently so the crabmeat does not fall apart. Form the mixture into 12 equal-size patties. Place the patties on a large baking sheet and refrigerate for at least 30 minutes.
2. Insert the Grill Grate and close the hood. Select Grill, set the temperature to HI, and set the time to 8 minutes. Select START/STOP to begin preheating.
3. When the unit beeps to signify it has preheated, spray avocado oil on both sides of 6 crab cakes and place them on the Grill Grate. Close the hood and cook for 4 minutes.
4. After 4 minutes, open the hood and flip the crab cakes. Close the hood and cook for 4 minutes more.
5. When cooking is complete, remove the crab cakes from the grill. Select GRILL, set the temperature to HI, and set the time to 8 minutes. Select START/STOP to begin and press PREHEAT to skip preheating. Repeat steps 3 and 4 for the remaining 6 crab cakes.
6. While the crab cakes are cooking, in a small bowl, combine the mayonnaise, garlic powder, lemon juice, and paprika. Feel free to add more lemon or a few dashes of hot sauce to adjust the taste to your liking.
7. When all of the crab cakes are cooked, serve with the sauce.

Crusted Codfish

Servings: 4

Cooking Time: 8 Minutes

Ingredients:

- 1 cup panko bread crumbs
- 2 tablespoons grated Parmesan cheese
- ¼ cup chopped pistachios
- 4 (4-ounce) frozen cod fillets, thawed
- 4 tablespoons Dijon mustard
- Cooking spray

Directions:

1. Insert the Grill Grate and close the hood. Select GRILL, set the temperature to HI, and set the time to 8 minutes. Select START/STOP to begin preheating.
2. While the unit is preheating, on a large plate, mix together the panko bread crumbs, Parmesan cheese, and pistachios. Evenly coat both sides of the cod fillets with the mustard, then press the fillets on the panko mixture on both sides to create a crust.
3. When the unit beeps to signify it has preheated, spray the crusted fillets with cooking spray and place them on the Grill Grate. Close the hood and grill for 4 minutes.
4. After 4 minutes, open the hood and flip the fillets. Close the hood and cook for 4 minutes more.
5. When cooking is complete, remove the fillets from the grill and serve.

BBQ Grill & Smoker Cookbook

Garlic Butter Shrimp Kebabs

Servings: 4

Cooking Time: 10 Minutes

Ingredients:

- 2 tablespoons unsalted butter, at room temperature
- 4 garlic cloves, minced
- 2 pounds jumbo shrimp, peeled
- 1 tablespoon garlic salt
- 1 teaspoon dried parsley

Directions:

1. Insert the Grill Grate. Place the butter and minced garlic in a heat-safe bowl, place the bowl on the Grill Grate, and close the hood. Select GRILL, set the temperature to HI, and set the time to 5 minutes. Select START/STOP to begin preheating. After 1 minute of preheating (set a separate timer), remove the bowl with the butter. Close the hood to continue preheating.
2. While the unit is preheating, place 4 or 5 shrimp on each of 8 skewers, with at least 1 inch left at the bottom. Place the skewers on a large plate. Lightly coat them with the garlic salt and parsley.
3. When the unit beeps to signify it has preheated, place 4 skewers on the Grill Grate. Brush some of the melted garlic butter on the shrimp. Close the hood and grill for 2 minutes, 30 seconds.
4. After 2 minutes, 30 seconds, open the hood and brush the shrimp with garlic butter again, then flip the skewers. Brush on more garlic butter. Close the hood and cook for 2 minutes, 30 seconds more.
5. When cooking is complete, the shrimp will be opaque and pink. Remove the skewers from the grill. Select GRILL, set the temperature to HI, and set the time to 5 minutes. Select START/STOP to begin and press PREHEAT to skip preheating. Repeat steps 3 and 4 for the remaining skewers. When all the skewers are cooked, serve.

Buttered Lobster Tails

Servings: 6

Cooking Time: 7 Minutes

Ingredients:

- 6 (4-ounce) lobster tails
- Paprika
- Salt
- Freshly ground black pepper
- 4 tablespoons (½ stick) unsalted butter, melted
- 3 garlic cloves, minced

Directions:

1. Place the lobster tails shell-side up on a cutting board. Using kitchen shears, cut each shell down the center, stopping at the base of the tail. Carefully crack open the shell by sliding your thumbs between the shell and meat and delicately pulling apart. Wiggle, pull, and lift the meat out of the shell. Remove the vein and digestive tract, if present. Rest the meat on top of the shell for a beautiful display.
2. Insert the Grill Grate and close the hood. Select GRILL, set the temperature to HI, and set the time to 7 minutes. Select START/STOP to begin preheating.
3. While the unit is preheating, season the lobster meat with paprika, salt, and pepper.
4. In a small bowl, combine the melted butter and garlic.
5. When the unit beeps to signify it has preheated, place the lobster tails on their shells on the Grill Grate. Close the hood and grill for 4 minutes.
6. After 4 minutes, open the hood and brush the garlic butter on the lobster meat. Close the hood and cook for 3 minutes more.
7. When cooking is complete, the lobster meat will be opaque and the shell will be orangey red. Serve with more melted butter or a sauce of your choice.

Lemon-garlic Butter Scallops

Servings: 6

Cooking Time: 4 Minutes

Ingredients:

- 2 pounds large sea scallops
- Salt
- Freshly ground black pepper
- 3 tablespoons avocado oil
- 3 garlic cloves, minced
- 8 tablespoons (1 stick) unsalted butter, sliced
- Juice of 1 lemon
- Chopped fresh parsley, for garnish

Directions:

1. Insert the Cooking Pot and close the hood. Select GRILL, set the temperature to HI, and set the time to 4 minutes. Select START/STOP to begin preheating.
2. While the unit is preheating, pat the scallops dry with a paper towel and season them with salt and pepper. After 5 minutes of preheating (set a separate timer), open the hood and add the avocado oil and garlic to the Cooking Pot, then close the hood to continue preheating.
3. When the unit beeps to signify it has preheated, use a spatula to spread the oil and garlic around the bottom of the Cooking Pot. Place the scallops in the pot in a single layer. Close the hood and cook for 2 minutes.
4. After 2 minutes, open the hood and flip the scallops. Add the butter to the pot and drizzle some lemon juice over each scallop. Close the hood and cook for 2 minutes more.
5. When cooking is complete, open the hood and flip the scallops again. Spoon melted garlic butter on top of each. The scallops should be slightly firm and opaque. Remove the scallops from the grill and serve, garnished with the parsley.

Lobster Rolls

Servings: 4

Cooking Time: 7 Minutes

Ingredients:

- ¼ cup mayonnaise
- Juice of ½ lemon
- ¼ teaspoon sea salt
- ⅛ teaspoon freshly ground black pepper
- 1 teaspoon dried parsley
- Dash paprika
- 1 pound frozen lobster meat, thawed, cut into 1-inch pieces
- Unsalted butter, at room temperature
- 4 sandwich rolls, such as French rolls, hoagie rolls, or large hot dog buns
- 1 lemon, cut into wedges

Directions:

1. Insert the Grill Grate and close the hood. Select GRILL, set the temperature to MED, and set the time to 7 minutes. Select START/STOP to begin preheating.
2. While the unit is preheating, in a large bowl, combine the mayonnaise, lemon juice, salt, pepper, parsley, and paprika.
3. When the unit beeps to signify it has preheated, place the lobster meat on the Grill Grate. Close the hood and grill for 4 minutes.
4. While the lobster is cooking, spread the butter on the sandwich rolls.
5. After 4 minutes, open the hood and remove the lobster meat. Set aside on a plate. Place the sandwich rolls on the grill, buttered-side down. Close the hood and grill for 2 minutes.
6. After 2 minutes, open the hood and flip the rolls. Close the hood and cook for 1 minute more.
7. When the bread is toasted and golden brown, remove it from the grill. Add the lobster meat to the mayonnaise mixture and gently fold in until well combined. Spoon the lobster meat into the sandwich rolls. Serve with the lemon wedges.

BBQ Grill & Smoker Cookbook

Coconut Shrimp With Orange Chili Sauce

Servings: 44

Cooking Time: 16 Minutes

Ingredients:

- For the coconut shrimp
- 2 large eggs
- 1 cup sweetened coconut flakes
- 1 cup panko bread crumbs
- ½ teaspoon salt
- ¼ teaspoon freshly ground black pepper
- 2 pounds jumbo shrimp, peeled
- For the orange chili sauce
- ½ cup orange marmalade
- 1 teaspoon sriracha or ¼ teaspoon red pepper flakes

Directions:

1. Insert the Grill Grate and close the hood. Select GRILL, set the temperature to HI, and set the time to 16 minutes. Select START/STOP to begin preheating.
2. While the unit is preheating, create an assembly line with 2 large bowls. In one bowl, whisk the eggs. In the other bowl, combine the coconut flakes, panko bread crumbs, salt, and pepper. One at a time, dip the shrimp in the egg and then into the coconut flakes until fully coated.
3. When the unit beeps to signify it has preheated, place half the shrimp on the Grill Grate in a single layer. Close the hood and cook for 4 minutes.
4. After 4 minutes, open the hood and flip the shrimp. Close the hood and cook for 4 minutes more. After 4 minutes, open the hood and remove the shrimp from the grill.
5. Repeat steps 3 and 4 for the remaining shrimp.
6. To make the orange chili sauce
7. In a small bowl, combine the orange marmalade and sriracha. Serve as a dipping sauce alongside the coconut shrimp.

Orange-ginger Soy Salmon

Servings: 4

Cooking Time: 12 Minutes

Ingredients:

- ½ cup low-sodium soy sauce
- ¼ cup orange marmalade
- 3 tablespoons light brown sugar, packed
- 1 tablespoon peeled minced fresh ginger
- 1 garlic clove, minced
- 4 (8-ounce) skin-on salmon fillets

Directions:

1. In a large bowl, whisk together the soy sauce, orange marmalade, brown sugar, ginger, and garlic until the sugar is dissolved. Set aside one-quarter of the marinade in a small bowl. Place the salmon fillets skin-side down in the marinade in the large bowl.
2. Insert the Grill Grate and close the hood. Select GRILL, set the temperature to MED, and set the time to 12 minutes. Select START/STOP to begin preheating.
3. When the unit beeps to signify it has preheated, place the salmon fillets on the Grill Grate, skin-side down. Spoon the remaining marinade in the large bowl over the fillets. Close the hood and cook for 10 minutes.
4. After 10 minutes, open the hood and brush the reserved marinade in the small bowl over the fillets. Close the hood and cook for 2 minutes more.
5. When cooking is complete, the salmon will be opaque and should flake easily with a fork. (If you want, you can also use the Smart Thermometer at the end of cooking to check that the internal temperature of the salmon has reached 145°F.) Remove the fillets from the grill and serve.

Striped Bass With Sesame-ginger Scallions

Servings: 4

Cooking Time: 8 Minutes

Ingredients:

- 4 (8-ounce) striped bass fillets
- Extra-virgin olive oil
- 2 (1-inch) pieces fresh ginger, peeled and thinly sliced
- ½ cup soy sauce
- ½ cup rice wine (mirin)
- 2 tablespoons sesame oil
- ¼ cup light brown sugar, packed
- ¼ cup water
- ¼ cup sliced scallions, both white and green parts, for garnish

Directions:

1. Insert the Cooking Pot and close the hood. Select GRILL, set the temperature to HI, and set the time to 8 minutes. Select START/STOP to begin preheating.
2. While the unit is preheating, drizzle the fish fillets with olive oil.
3. When the unit beeps to signify it has preheated, place the fillets in the Cooking Pot in a single layer. Place the ginger slices on top of the fillets. Close the hood and cook for 6 minutes.
4. While the fish is cooking, in a small bowl, whisk together the soy sauce, rice wine, sesame oil, brown sugar, and water until the sugar dissolves.
5. After 6 minutes, open the hood and pour the soy sauce mixture over the fish. Close the hood and cook for 2 minutes more.
6. When cooking is complete, open the hood and remove the fillets from the grill. Garnish with the scallions and serve.

Halibut With Lemon And Capers

Servings: 4

Cooking Time: 8 Minutes

Ingredients:

- 4 halibut steaks (at least 1 inch thick)
- Extra-virgin olive oil
- 1 lemon
- 1 cup white wine
- 3 garlic cloves, minced
- 4 tablespoons capers
- 4 tablespoons (½ stick) unsalted butter, sliced

Directions:

1. Insert the Cooking Pot and close the hood. Select GRILL, set the temperature to HI, and set the time to 8 minutes. Select START/STOP to begin preheating.
2. While the unit is preheating, drizzle the fish fillets with olive oil. Cut half the lemon into thin slices and place them on top of the fillets.
3. When the unit beeps to signify it has preheated, place the fillets in the Cooking Pot. Close the hood and cook for 4 minutes.
4. After 4 minutes, open the hood and add the white wine. Close the hood and cook for 2 minutes. After 2 minutes, open the hood and add the garlic, capers, and butter. Squeeze the juice of the remaining ½ lemon over the fish. Close the hood and cook for 2 minutes more.
5. When cooking is complete, open the hood and spoon the sauce over the fish. If the capers have not popped, give about half of them a tap with the spoon to pop them. Stir the sauce and serve with the fillets.

Tomato-stuffed Grilled Sole

Servings: 6

Cooking Time: 7 Minutes

Ingredients:

- 6 tablespoons mayonnaise
- 1 teaspoon garlic powder
- 1 (14-ounce) can diced tomatoes, drained
- 6 (4-ounce) sole fillets
- Cooking spray
- 6 tablespoons panko bread crumbs

Directions:

1. Insert the Grill Grate and close the hood. Select GRILL, set the temperature to HI, and set the time to 7 minutes. Select START/STOP to begin preheating.
2. While the unit is preheating, in a small bowl, combine the mayonnaise and garlic powder. Slowly fold in the tomatoes, making sure to be gentle so they don't turn to mush. Place the sole fillets on a large, flat surface and spread the mayonnaise across the top of each. Roll up the fillets, creating pinwheels. Spray the top of each roll with cooking spray, then press 1 tablespoon of panko bread crumbs on top of each.
3. When the unit beeps to signify it has preheated, place the fillets on the Grill Grate, seam-side down. Close the hood and grill for 7 minutes.
4. When cooking is complete, the panko bread crumbs will be crisp, and the fish will have turned opaque. Remove the fish from the grill and serve.

Tilapia With Cilantro And Ginger

Servings: 4

Cooking Time: 8 Minutes

Ingredients:

- Extra-virgin olive oil
- 4 (8-ounce) tilapia fillets
- 2 tablespoons soy sauce
- 1 teaspoon sesame oil
- 1 tablespoon honey
- 1 tablespoon peeled minced fresh ginger
- ½ cup chopped fresh cilantro

Directions:

1. Insert the Cooking Pot and close the hood. Select GRILL, set the temperature to HI, and set the time to 8 minutes. Select START/STOP to begin preheating.
2. While the unit is preheating, drizzle the fish fillets with olive oil.
3. When the unit beeps to signify it has preheated, place the fillets in the Cooking Pot in a single layer. Close the hood and cook for 6 minutes.
4. While the fish is cooking, in a small bowl, whisk together the soy sauce, sesame oil, honey, ginger, and cilantro.
5. After 6 minutes, open the hood and pour the sauce over the fillets. Close the hood and cook for 2 minutes more.
6. When cooking is complete, remove the fillets from the grill and serve.

Desserts

BBQ Grill & Smoker Cookbook

Desserts

Cinnamon Candied Apples

Servings: 4

Cooking Time: 12 Minutes

Ingredients:

- 1 cup packed light brown sugar
- 2 teaspoons ground cinnamon
- 2 medium Granny Smith apples, peeled and diced

Directions:

1. Select BAKE, set the temperature to 350°F, and set the time to 12 minutes. Select START/STOP to begin preheating.
2. Thoroughly combine the brown sugar and cinnamon in a medium bowl.
3. Add the apples to the bowl and stir until well coated. Transfer the apples to a baking pan.
4. Place the pan directly in the pot. Close the hood and BAKE for 9 minutes. Stir the apples once and bake for an additional 3 minutes until softened.
5. Serve warm.

Chocolate Pecan Pie

Servings: 8

Cooking Time: 25 Minutes

Ingredients:

- 1 unbaked pie crust
- Filling:
- 2 large eggs
- ⅓ cup butter, melted
- 1 cup sugar
- ½ cup all-purpose flour
- 1 cup milk chocolate chips
- 1½ cups coarsely chopped pecans
- 2 tablespoons bourbon

Directions:

1. Select BAKE, set the temperature to 350°F, and set the time to 25 minutes. Select START/STOP to begin preheating.
2. Whisk the eggs and melted butter in a large bowl until creamy.
3. Add the sugar and flour and stir to incorporate. Mix in the milk chocolate chips, pecans, and bourbon and stir until well combined.
4. Use a fork to prick holes in the bottom and sides of the pie crust. Pour the prepared filling into the pie crust. Place the pie crust in the pot.
5. Close the hood and BAKE for 25 minutes until a toothpick inserted in the center comes out clean.
6. Allow the pie cool for 10 minutes in the basket before serving.

Banana And Walnut Cake

Servings: 6

Cooking Time: 25 Minutes

Ingredients:

- 1 pound bananas, mashed
- 8 ounces flour
- 6 ounces sugar
- 3.5 ounces walnuts, chopped
- 2.5 ounces butter, melted
- 2 eggs, lightly beaten
- ¼ teaspoon baking soda

Directions:

1. Select BAKE, set the temperature to 355°F, and set the time to 10 minutes. Select START/STOP to begin preheating.
2. In a bowl, combine the sugar, butter, egg, flour, and baking soda with a whisk. Stir in the bananas and walnuts.
3. Transfer the mixture to a greased baking pan. Place the pan directly in the pot. Close the hood and BAKE for 10 minutes.
4. Reduce the temperature to 330°F and bake for another 15 minutes. Serve hot.

BBQ Grill & Smoker Cookbook

Sweet Potato Donuts

Servings: 12

Cooking Time: 52 Minutes

Ingredients:

- 3 cups water
- 1 medium white sweet potato
- ⅔ cup all-purpose flour, plus more for dusting
- ½ cup granulated sugar
- Avocado oil

Directions:

1. Insert the Cooking Pot, pour in the water, and close the hood. Select BROIL, set the temperature to 500°F, and set the time to 20 minutes. Select START/STOP to begin preheating.
2. While the unit is preheating, peel the sweet potato and cut it into chunks.
3. When the unit beeps to signify it has preheated, add the sweet potato to the Cooking Pot, making sure the chunks are fully submerged in the water. Close the hood and cook for 20 minutes.
4. After 20 minutes, open the hood and pierce a potato chunk to check for doneness—it should be easy to slice into. Remove and drain the sweet potatoes.
5. In a large bowl, mash the sweet potato with a masher or fork. When it has cooled down, add ⅔ cup of flour and the sugar and mix until well combined. The dough will be sticky. Dust a clean work surface with some flour. Roll and knead the dough until it is no longer sticky and holds its form, using more flour as needed.
6. Divide the dough in half and then cut each half into 6 equal-size pieces. Roll each piece of dough into a cylinder about 4 inches long.
7. Insert the Cooking Pot and close the hood. Select GRILL, set the temperature to HI, and set the time to 16 minutes. Select START/STOP to begin preheating.
8. While the unit is preheating, brush avocado oil on a 6-ring donut pan and place 6 donuts in the molds. Brush more avocado oil on top.
9. When the unit beeps to signify it has preheated, place the donut pan in the Cooking Pot. Close the hood and grill for 8 minutes.
10. When cooking is complete, remove the pan and transfer the donuts to a rack to cool.
11. Repeat steps 8 through 10 with the remaining donuts. Serve.

Fresh Blueberry Cobbler

Servings: 6

Cooking Time: 30 Minutes

Ingredients:

- 4 cups fresh blueberries
- 1 teaspoon grated lemon zest
- 1 cup sugar, plus 2 tablespoons
- 1 cup all-purpose flour, plus 2 tablespoons
- Juice of 1 lemon
- 2 teaspoons baking powder
- ¼ teaspoon salt
- 6 tablespoons unsalted butter
- ¾ cup whole milk
- ⅛ teaspoon ground cinnamon

Directions:

1. In a medium bowl, combine the blueberries, lemon zest, 2 tablespoons of sugar, 2 tablespoons of flour, and lemon juice.
2. In a medium bowl, combine the remaining 1 cup of flour and 1 cup of sugar, baking powder, and salt. Cut the butter into the flour mixture until it forms an even crumb texture. Stir in the milk until a dough forms.
3. Select BAKE, set the temperature to 350°F, and set the time to 30 minutes. Select START/STOP to begin preheating.
4. Meanwhile, pour the blueberry mixture into the baking pan, spreading it evenly across the pan. Gently pour the batter over the blueberry mixture, then sprinkle the cinnamon over the top.
5. When the unit beeps to signify it has preheated, place the pan directly in the pot. Close the hood and BAKE for 30 minutes, until lightly golden.
6. When cooking is complete, serve warm.

BBQ Grill & Smoker Cookbook

Lemon Squares

Servings: 4

Cooking Time: 35 Minutes

Ingredients:

- 1 cup all-purpose flour
- 8 tablespoons (1 stick) unsalted butter, at room temperature
- ⅓ cup powdered sugar, plus additional for dusting
- 2 large eggs
- ⅔ cup granulated sugar
- ½ teaspoon baking powder
- ¼ teaspoon salt
- Juice of 1 lemon

Directions:

1. Insert the Cooking Pot and close the hood. Select BAKE, set the temperature to 325°F, and set the time to 35 minutes. Select START/STOP to begin preheating.
2. While the unit is preheating, in a large bowl, combine the flour, butter, and powdered sugar. Use your hands to smash and mix until the mixture has a crumbly texture. Transfer the mixture to a 6-inch square pan, using your fingers to press the dough into the bottom of the pan to form a crust.
3. When the unit beeps to signify it has preheated, place the pan in the Cooking Pot. Close the hood and cook for 5 minutes.
4. While the crust is baking, in a small bowl, beat the eggs, then add the sugar, baking powder, salt, and lemon juice and mix until well combined.
5. After 5 minutes, open the hood and pour the lemon filling over the crust. Cover the pan with aluminum foil (use grill mitts), making sure the foil tucks under the bottom of the pan so it does not lift up and block the Splatter Shield as the air flows while baking. Close the hood and cook for 20 minutes.
6. After 20 minutes, open the hood and remove the foil. Close the hood and bake uncovered for 10 minutes more.
7. When cooking is complete, remove the pan and let cool for at least 1 to 2 hours. Dust with additional powdered sugar and serve.

Everyday Cheesecake

Servings: 4

Cooking Time: 35 Minutes

Ingredients:

- 1 large egg
- 8 ounces cream cheese, at room temperature
- ¼ cup heavy (whipping) cream
- ¼ cup sour cream
- ¼ cup powdered sugar
- 1 teaspoon vanilla extract
- 5 ounces cookies, such as chocolate, vanilla, cinnamon, or your favorite
- 4 tablespoons (½ stick) unsalted butter, melted

Directions:

1. In a large bowl, whisk the egg. Then add the cream cheese, heavy cream, and sour cream and whisk until smooth. Slowly add the powdered sugar and vanilla, whisking until fully mixed.
2. Insert the Cooking Pot and close the hood. Select BAKE, set the temperature to 350°F, and set the time to 35 minutes. Select START/STOP to begin preheating.
3. While the unit is preheating, crush the cookies into fine crumbs. Place them in a 6-inch springform pan and drizzle evenly with the melted butter. Using your fingers, press down on the crumbs to form a crust on the bottom of the pan. Pour the cream cheese mixture on top of the crust. Cover the pan with aluminum foil, making sure the foil fully covers the sides of the pan and tucks under the bottom so it does not lift up and block the Splatter Shield as the air flows while baking.
4. When the unit beeps to signify it has preheated, place the springform pan in the Cooking Pot. Close the hood and cook for 25 minutes.
5. After 25 minutes, open the hood and remove the foil. Close the hood and cook for 10 minutes more.
6. When cooking is complete, remove the pan from the Cooking Pot and let the cheesecake cool for 1 hour, then place the cheesecake in the refrigerator for at least 3 hours. Slice and serve.

Black And White Brownies

Servings: 1

Cooking Time: 20 Minutes

Ingredients:

- 1 egg
- ¼ cup brown sugar
- 2 tablespoons white sugar
- 2 tablespoons safflower oil
- 1 teaspoon vanilla
- ⅓ cup all-purpose flour
- ¼ cup cocoa powder
- ¼ cup white chocolate chips
- Nonstick cooking spray

Directions:

1. Select BAKE, set the temperature to 340°F, and set the time to 20 minutes. Select START/STOP to begin preheating.
2. Spritz a baking pan with nonstick cooking spray.
3. Whisk together the egg, brown sugar, and white sugar in a medium bowl. Mix in the safflower oil and vanilla and stir to combine.
4. Add the flour and cocoa powder and stir just until incorporated. Fold in the white chocolate chips.
5. Scrape the batter into the prepared baking pan.
6. Place the pan directly in the pot. Close the hood and BAKE for 20 minutes, or until the brownie springs back when touched lightly with your fingers.
7. Transfer to a wire rack and let cool for 30 minutes before slicing to serve.

Lemony Blackberry Crisp

Servings: 1

Cooking Time: 20 Minutes

Ingredients:

- 2 tablespoons lemon juice
- ⅓ cup powdered erythritol
- ¼ teaspoon xantham gum
- 2 cup blackberries
- 1 cup crunchy granola

Directions:

1. Select BAKE, set the temperature to 350°F, and set the time to 15 minutes. Select START/STOP to begin preheating.
2. In a bowl, combine the lemon juice, erythritol, xantham gum, and blackberries. Transfer to a round baking pan and cover with aluminum foil.
3. Place the pan directly in the pot. Close the hood and BAKE for 12 minutes.
4. Take care when removing the pan from the grill. Give the blackberries a stir and top with the granola.
5. Return the pan to the grill and bake at 320°F for an additional 3 minutes. Serve once the granola has turned brown and enjoy.

Lemon Ricotta Cake

Servings: 6

Cooking Time: 25 Minutes

Ingredients:

- 17.5 ounces ricotta cheese
- 5.4 ounces sugar
- 3 eggs, beaten
- 3 tablespoons flour
- 1 lemon, juiced and zested
- 2 teaspoons vanilla extract

Directions:

1. Select BAKE, set the temperature to 320°F, and set the time to 25 minutes. Select START/STOP to begin preheating.
2. In a large mixing bowl, stir together all the ingredients until the mixture reaches a creamy consistency.
3. Pour the mixture into a baking pan. Place the pan directly in the pot.
4. Close the hood and BAKE for 25 minutes until a toothpick inserted in the center comes out clean.
5. Allow to cool for 10 minutes on a wire rack before serving.

Chia Pudding

Servings: 2

Cooking Time: 4 Minutes

Ingredients:

- 1 cup chia seeds
- 1 cup unsweetened coconut milk
- 1 teaspoon liquid stevia
- 1 tablespoon coconut oil
- 1 teaspoon butter, melted

Directions:

1. Select BAKE, set the temperature to 360°F, and set the time to 4 minutes. Select START/STOP to begin preheating.
2. Mix together the chia seeds, coconut milk, and stevia in a large bowl. Add the coconut oil and melted butter and stir until well blended.
3. Divide the mixture evenly between the ramekins, filling only about ⅔ of the way. Transfer to the pot.
4. Close the hood and BAKE for 4 minutes.
5. Allow to cool for 5 minutes and serve warm.

Marshmallow Banana Boat

Servings: 4

Cooking Time: 6 Minutes

Ingredients:

- 4 ripe bananas
- 1 cup mini marshmallows
- ½ cup chocolate chips
- ½ cup peanut butter chips

Directions:

1. Insert the Grill Grate and close the hood. Select GRILL, set the temperature to MEDIUM, and set the time to 6 minutes. Select START/STOP to begin preheating.
2. While the unit is preheating, slice each banana lengthwise while still in its peel, making sure not to cut all the way through. Using both hands, pull the banana peel open like you would a book, revealing the banana inside. Divide the marshmallows, chocolate chips, and peanut butter chips among the bananas, stuffing them inside the skin.
3. When the unit beeps to signify it has preheated, place the stuffed banana on the Grill Grate. Close the hood and GRILL for 4 to 6 minutes, until the chocolate is melted and the marshmallows are toasted.

Graham Cracker Cheesecake

Servings: 8

Cooking Time: 20 Minutes

Ingredients:

- 1 cup graham cracker crumbs
- 3 tablespoons softened butter
- 1½ packages cream cheese, softened
- ⅓ cup sugar
- 2 eggs
- 1 tablespoon flour
- 1 teaspoon vanilla
- ¼ cup chocolate syrup

Directions:

1. For the crust, combine the graham cracker crumbs and butter in a small bowl and mix well. Press into the bottom of a baking pan and put in the freezer to set.
2. For the filling, combine the cream cheese and sugar in a medium bowl and mix well. Beat in the eggs, one at a time. Add the flour and vanilla.
3. Select BAKE, set the temperature to 450°F, and set the time to 20 minutes. Select START/STOP to begin preheating.
4. Remove ⅔ cup of the filling to a small bowl and stir in the chocolate syrup until combined.
5. Pour the vanilla filling into the pan with the crust. Drop the chocolate filling over the vanilla filling by the spoonful. With a clean butter knife, stir the fillings in a zigzag pattern to marbleize them.
6. Place the pan directly in the pot. Close the hood and BAKE for 20 minutes or until the cheesecake is just set.
7. Cool on a wire rack for 1 hour, then chill in the refrigerator until the cheesecake is firm.
8. Serve immediately.

Vanilla Scones

Servings: 18

Cooking Time: 15 Minutes

Ingredients:

- For the scones
- 2 cups almond flour
- ¼ cup granulated sugar
- ¼ teaspoon salt
- 1 tablespoon baking powder
- 2 large eggs
- 1 teaspoon vanilla extract
- 4 tablespoons (½ stick) unsalted butter, melted
- 2 tablespoons heavy (whipping) cream
- For the icing
- 1 cup powdered sugar
- 2 tablespoons heavy (whipping) cream
- 1 tablespoon vanilla extract

Directions:

1. In a large bowl, combine the almond flour, granulated sugar, salt, and baking powder. In another large bowl, whisk the eggs, then whisk in the vanilla, butter, and heavy cream. Add the dry ingredients to the wet and mix just until a dough forms.
2. Insert the Cooking Pot and close the hood. Select BAKE, set the temperature to 325°F, and set the time to 15 minutes. Select START/STOP to begin preheating.
3. While the unit is preheating, divide the dough into 3 equal pieces. Shape each piece into a disc about 1 inch thick and 5 inches in diameter. Cut each into 6 wedges, like slicing a pizza.
4. When the unit beeps to signify it has preheated, place the scones in the Cooking Pot, spacing them apart so they don't bake together. Close the hood and cook for 15 minutes.
5. While the scones are baking, in a small bowl, combine the powdered sugar, heavy cream, and vanilla. Stir until smooth.
6. After 15 minutes, open the hood and remove the scones. They are done baking when they have turned a light golden brown. Place on a wire rack to cool to room temperature. Drizzle the icing over the scones, or pour a tablespoonful on the top of each scone for an even glaze.

Strawberry Pizza

Servings: 4

Cooking Time: 6 Minutes

Ingredients:

- 2 tablespoons all-purpose flour, plus more as needed
- ½ store-bought pizza dough
- 1 tablespoon canola oil
- 1 cup sliced fresh strawberries
- 1 tablespoon sugar
- ½ cup chocolate-hazelnut spread

Directions:

1. Insert the Grill Grate and close the hood. Select GRILL, set the temperature to MAX, and set the time to 6 minutes. Select START/STOP to begin preheating.
2. While the unit is preheating, dust a clean work surface with the flour. Place the dough on the floured surface, and roll it out to a 9-inch round of even thickness. Dust your rolling pin and work surface with additional flour, as needed, to ensure the dough does not stick.
3. Brush the surface of the rolled-out dough evenly with half the oil. Flip the dough over, and brush with the remaining oil. Poke the dough with a fork 5 or 6 times across its surface to prevent air pockets from forming during cooking.
4. When the unit beeps to signify it has preheated, place the dough on the Grill Grate. Close the hood and GRILL for 3 minutes.
5. After 3 minutes, flip the dough. Close the hood and continue grilling for the remaining 3 minutes.
6. Meanwhile, in a medium mixing bowl, combine the strawberries and sugar.
7. Transfer the pizza to a cutting board and let cool. Top with the chocolate-hazelnut spread and strawberries. Cut into pieces and serve.

Easy Blackberry Cobbler

Servings: 6

Cooking Time: 25 To 30 Minutes

Ingredients:

- 3 cups fresh or frozen blackberries
- 1¾ cups sugar, divided
- 1 teaspoon vanilla extract
- 8 tablespoons butter, melted
- 1 cup self-rising flour
- Cooking spray

Directions:

1. Select BAKE, set the temperature to 350°F, and set the time to 30 minutes. Select START/STOP to begin preheating.
2. Spritz a baking pan with cooking spray.
3. Mix the blackberries, 1 cup of sugar, and vanilla in a medium bowl and stir to combine.
4. Stir together the melted butter, remaining sugar, and flour in a separate medium bowl.
5. Spread the blackberry mixture evenly in the prepared pan and top with the butter mixture.
6. Place the pan directly in the pot. Close the hood and BAKE for 20 to 25 minutes. Check for doneness and bake for another 5 minutes, if needed.
7. Remove from the grill and place on a wire rack to cool to room temperature. Serve immediately.

Rum Grilled Pineapple Sundaes

Servings: 6

Cooking Time: 8 Minutes

Ingredients:

- ½ cup dark rum
- ½ cup packed brown sugar
- 1 teaspoon ground cinnamon, plus more for garnish
- 1 pineapple, cored and sliced
- Vanilla ice cream, for serving

Directions:

1. In a large shallow bowl or storage container, combine the rum, sugar, and cinnamon. Add the pineapple slices and arrange them in a single layer. Coat with the mixture, then let soak for at least 5 minutes per side.
2. Insert the Grill Grate and close the hood. Select GRILL, set the temperature to MAX, and set the time to 8 minutes. Select START/STOP to begin preheating.
3. While the unit is preheating, strain the extra rum sauce from the pineapple.
4. When the unit beeps to signify it has preheated, place the fruit on the Grill Grate in a single layer (you may need to do this in multiple batches). Gently press the fruit down to maximize grill marks. Close the hood and GRILL for about 6 to 8 minutes without flipping. If working in batches, remove the pineapple, and repeat this step for the remaining pineapple slices.
5. When cooking is complete, remove, and top each pineapple ring with a scoop of ice cream. Sprinkle with cinnamon and serve immediately.

Pumpkin Pudding

Servings: 4

Cooking Time: 15 Minutes

Ingredients:

- 3 cups pumpkin purée
- 3 tablespoons honey
- 1 tablespoon ginger
- 1 tablespoon cinnamon
- 1 teaspoon clove
- 1 teaspoon nutmeg
- 1 cup full-fat cream
- 2 eggs
- 1 cup sugar

Directions:

1. Select BAKE, set the temperature to 390°F, and set the time to 15 minutes. Select START/STOP to begin preheating.
2. In a bowl, stir all the ingredients together to combine.
3. Scrape the mixture into a greased baking pan. Place the pan directly in the pot. Close the hood and BAKE for 15 minutes.
4. Serve warm.

Churros With Chocolate-yogurt Sauce

Servings: 8

Cooking Time: 30 Minutes

Ingredients:

- 1 cup water
- 1 stick unsalted butter, cut into 8 pieces
- ½ cup sugar, plus 1 tablespoon
- 1 cup all-purpose flour
- 1 teaspoon vanilla extract
- 3 large eggs
- 2 teaspoons ground cinnamon
- Nonstick cooking spray
- 4 ounces dark chocolate, chopped
- ¼ cup Greek yogurt

Directions:

1. In a medium saucepan over medium-high heat, combine the water, butter, and the 1 tablespoon of sugar. Bring to a simmer. Add the flour, stirring it in quickly. Continue to cook, stirring constantly, until the mixture is thick, about 3 minutes. Transfer to a large bowl.
2. Using a spoon, beat the flour mixture for about 1 minute, until cooled slightly. Stir in the vanilla, then the eggs, one at a time.
3. Transfer the dough to a plastic bag or a piping bag. Let the dough rest for 1 hour at room temperature.
4. Insert the Crisper Basket and close the hood. Select AIR CRISP, set the temperature to 375ºF, and set the time to 30 minutes. Select START/STOP to begin preheating.
5. Meanwhile, in a medium shallow bowl, combine the cinnamon and remaining ½ cup of sugar.
6. When the unit beeps to signify it has preheated, spray the basket with the nonstick cooking spray. Take the plastic bag with your dough and cut off one corner. Pipe the batter directly into the Crisper Basket, making 6 churros, placed at least ½ inch apart. Close the hood and AIR CRISP for 10 minutes.
7. Meanwhile, in a small microwave-safe mixing bowl, melt the chocolate in the microwave, stirring it after every 30 seconds, until completely melted and smooth. Add the yogurt and whisk until smooth.
8. After 10 minutes, carefully transfer the churros to the sugar mixture and toss to coat evenly. Repeat piping and air crisping with the remaining batter, adding time as needed.
9. Serve the churros with the warm chocolate dipping sauce.

Orange Cake

Servings: 8

Cooking Time: 23 Minutes

Ingredients:

- Nonstick baking spray with flour
- 1¼ cups all-purpose flour
- ⅓ cup yellow cornmeal
- ¾ cup white sugar
- 1 teaspoon baking soda
- ¼ cup safflower oil
- 1¼ cups orange juice, divided
- 1 teaspoon vanilla
- ¼ cup powdered sugar

Directions:

1. Select BAKE, set the temperature to 350ºF, and set the time to 23 minutes. Select START/STOP to begin preheating.
2. Spray a baking pan with nonstick spray and set aside.
3. In a medium bowl, combine the flour, cornmeal, sugar, baking soda, safflower oil, 1 cup of the orange juice, and vanilla, and mix well.
4. Pour the batter into the baking pan. Place the pan directly in the pot. Close the hood and BAKE for 23 minutes or until a toothpick inserted in the center of the cake comes out clean.
5. Remove the cake from the grill and place on a cooling rack. Using a toothpick, make about 20 holes in the cake.
6. In a small bowl, combine remaining ¼ cup of orange juice and the powdered sugar and stir well. Drizzle this mixture over the hot cake slowly so the cake absorbs it.
7. Cool completely, then cut into wedges to serve.

Apple, Peach, And Cranberry Crisp

Servings: 8

Cooking Time: 12 Minutes

Ingredients:

- 1 apple, peeled and chopped
- 2 peaches, peeled and chopped
- ⅓ cup dried cranberries
- 2 tablespoons honey
- ⅓ cup brown sugar
- ¼ cup flour
- ½ cup oatmeal
- 3 tablespoons softened butter

Directions:

1. Select BAKE, set the temperature to 370ºF, and set the time to 12 minutes. Select START/STOP to begin preheating.
2. In a baking pan, combine the apple, peaches, cranberries, and honey, and mix well.
3. In a medium bowl, combine the brown sugar, flour, oatmeal, and butter, and mix until crumbly. Sprinkle this mixture over the fruit in the pan.
4. Place the pan directly in the pot. Close the hood and BAKE for 10 to 12 minutes or until the fruit is bubbly and the topping is golden brown. Serve warm.

Fudge Pie

Servings: 8

Cooking Time: 25 To 30 Minutes

Ingredients:

- 1½ cups sugar
- ½ cup self-rising flour
- ⅓ cup unsweetened cocoa powder
- 3 large eggs, beaten
- 12 tablespoons butter, melted
- 1½ teaspoons vanilla extract
- 1 unbaked pie crust
- ¼ cup confectioners' sugar (optional)

Directions:

1. Select BAKE, set the temperature to 350ºF, and set the time to 30 minutes. Select START/STOP to begin preheating.
2. Thoroughly combine the sugar, flour, and cocoa powder in a medium bowl. Add the beaten eggs and butter and whisk to combine. Stir in the vanilla.
3. Pour the prepared filling into the pie crust and transfer to the pot.
4. Close the hood and BAKE for 25 to 30 minutes until just set.
5. Allow the pie to cool for 5 minutes. Sprinkle with the confectioners' sugar, if desired. Serve warm.

Pound Cake With Mixed Berries

Servings: 6

Cooking Time: 8 Minutes

Ingredients:

- 3 tablespoons unsalted butter, at room temperature
- 6 slices pound cake, sliced about 1-inch thick
- 1 cup fresh raspberries
- 1 cup fresh blueberries
- 3 tablespoons sugar
- ½ tablespoon fresh mint, minced

Directions:

1. Insert the Grill Grate and close the hood. Select GRILL, set the temperature to MAX, and set the time to 8 minutes. Select START/STOP to begin preheating.
2. While the unit is preheating, evenly spread the butter on both sides of each slice of pound cake.
3. When the unit beeps to signify it has preheated, place the pound cake on the Grill Grate. Close the hood and GRILL for 2 minutes.
4. After 2 minutes, flip the pound cake and GRILL for 2 minutes more, until golden brown. Repeat steps 3 and 4 for all of the pound cake slices.
5. While the pound cake grills, in a medium mixing bowl, combine the raspberries, blueberries, sugar, and mint.
6. When cooking is complete, plate the cake slices and serve topped with the berry mixture.

BBQ Grill & Smoker Cookbook

Rich Chocolate Cookie

Servings: 4

Cooking Time: 9 Minutes

Ingredients:

- Nonstick baking spray with flour
- 3 tablespoons softened butter
- ⅓ cup plus 1 tablespoon brown sugar
- 1 egg yolk
- ½ cup flour
- 2 tablespoons ground white chocolate
- ¼ teaspoon baking soda
- ½ teaspoon vanilla
- ¾ cup chocolate chips

Directions:

1. Select BAKE, set the temperature to 350ºF, and set the time to 9 minutes. Select START/STOP to begin preheating.
2. In a medium bowl, beat the butter and brown sugar together until fluffy. Stir in the egg yolk.
3. Add the flour, white chocolate, baking soda, and vanilla, and mix well. Stir in the chocolate chips.
4. Line a baking pan with parchment paper. Spray the parchment paper with nonstick baking spray with flour.
5. Spread the batter into the prepared pan, leaving a ½-inch border on all sides.
6. Place the pan directly in the pot. Close the hood and BAKE for 9 minutes or until the cookie is light brown and just barely set.
7. Remove the pan from the grill and let cool for 10 minutes. Remove the cookie from the pan, remove the parchment paper, and let cool on a wire rack.
8. Serve immediately.

Chocolate S'mores

Servings: 12

Cooking Time: 3 Minutes

Ingredients:

- 12 whole cinnamon graham crackers
- 2 chocolate bars, broken into 12 pieces
- 12 marshmallows

Directions:

1. Insert the Crisper Basket and close the hood. Select BAKE, set the temperature to 350ºF, and set the time to 3 minutes. Select START/STOP to begin preheating.
2. Halve each graham cracker into 2 squares.
3. Put 6 graham cracker squares in the basket. Do not stack. Put a piece of chocolate into each. Close the hood and BAKE for 2 minutes.
4. Open the grill and add a marshmallow onto each piece of melted chocolate. Bake for 1 additional minute.
5. Remove the cooked s'mores from the grill, then repeat steps 2 and 3 for the remaining 6 s'mores.
6. Top with the remaining graham cracker squares and serve.

Peaches-and-cake Skewers

Servings: 4

Cooking Time: 8 Minutes

Ingredients:

- 1 loaf pound cake, cut into 1-inch cubes
- 4 peaches, sliced
- ½ cup condensed milk

Directions:

1. Insert the Grill Grate and close the hood. Select GRILL, set the temperature to HI, and set the time to 8 minutes. Select START/STOP to begin preheating.
2. While the unit is preheating, alternate cake cubes and peach slices, 3 or 4 pieces of each, on each of 12 skewers. Using a basting brush, brush the condensed milk onto the cake and peaches and place the skewers on a plate or baking sheet.
3. When the unit beeps to signify it has preheated, place 6 skewers on the Grill Grate. Close the hood and cook for 2 minutes.
4. After 2 minutes, open the hood and flip the skewers. Close the hood to cook for 2 minutes more.
5. After 2 minutes, open the hood and remove the skewers. Repeat steps 3 and 4 with the remaining 6 skewers. Serve.

BBQ Grill & Smoker Cookbook

Coffee Chocolate Cake

Servings: 8

Cooking Time: 30 Minutes

Ingredients:

- Dry Ingredients:
- 1½ cups almond flour
- ½ cup coconut meal
- ⅔ cup Swerve
- 1 teaspoon baking powder
- ¼ teaspoon salt
- Wet Ingredients:
- 1 egg
- 1 stick butter, melted
- ½ cup hot strongly brewed coffee
- Topping:
- ½ cup confectioner's Swerve
- ¼ cup coconut flour
- 3 tablespoons coconut oil
- 1 teaspoon ground cinnamon
- ½ teaspoon ground cardamom

Directions:

1. Select BAKE, set the temperature to 330°F, and set the time to 30 minutes. Select START/STOP to begin preheating.
2. In a medium bowl, combine the almond flour, coconut meal, Swerve, baking powder, and salt.
3. In a large bowl, whisk the egg, melted butter, and coffee until smooth.
4. Add the dry mixture to the wet and stir until well incorporated. Transfer the batter to a greased baking pan.
5. Stir together all the ingredients for the topping in a small bowl. Spread the topping over the batter and smooth the top with a spatula.
6. Place the pan directly in the pot. Close the hood and BAKE for 30 minutes, or until the cake springs back when gently pressed with your fingers.
7. Rest for 10 minutes before serving.

Ultimate Skillet Brownies

Servings: 6

Cooking Time: 40 Minutes

Ingredients:

- ½ cup all-purpose flour
- ¼ cup unsweetened cocoa powder
- ¾ teaspoon sea salt
- 2 large eggs
- 1 tablespoon water
- ½ cup granulated sugar
- ½ cup dark brown sugar
- 1 tablespoon vanilla extract
- 8 ounces semisweet chocolate chips, melted
- ¾ cup unsalted butter, melted
- Nonstick cooking spray

Directions:

1. In a medium bowl, whisk together the flour, cocoa powder, and salt.
2. In a large bowl, whisk together the eggs, water, sugar, brown sugar, and vanilla until smooth.
3. In a microwave-safe bowl, melt the chocolate in the microwave. In a separate microwave-safe bowl, melt the butter.
4. In a separate medium bowl, stir together the chocolate and butter until evenly combined. Whisk into the egg mixture. Then slowly add the dry ingredients, stirring just until incorporated.
5. Remove the Grill Grate from the unit. Select BAKE, set the temperature to 350°F, and set the time to 40 minutes. Select START/STOP to begin preheating.
6. Meanwhile, lightly grease the baking pan with cooking spray. Pour the batter into the pan, spreading evenly.
7. When the unit beeps to signify it has preheated, place the pan directly in the pot. Close the hood and BAKE for 40 minutes.
8. After 40 minutes, check that baking is complete. A wooden toothpick inserted into the center of the brownies should come out clean.

How can you tackle late night snacking and curb unhealthy choices?

Eat balanced meals for dinner.

Establish regular meal times.

Drink water or herbal tea.

Choose healthy snacks like fruits or veggies.

Portion control to avoid overeating.

Practice mindful eating.

Remove unhealthy snacks from your home.

Find distractions or hobbies.

Prioritize quality sleep.

Seek accountability from a friend.

Opt for healthier snack options.

MEASUREMENT CONVERSIONS

BASIC KITCHEN CONVERSIONS & EQUIVALENT

DRY MEASUREMENTS CONVERSION CHART

3 TEASPOONS = 1 TABLESPOON = 1/16 CUP

6 TEASPOONS = 2 TABLESPOONS = 1/8 CUP

12 TEASPOONS = 4 TABLESPOONS = 1/4 CUP

24 TEASPOONS = 8 TABLESPOONS = 1/2 CUP

36 TEASPOONS = 12 TABLESPOONS = 3/4 CUP

48 TEASPOONS = 16 TABLESPOONS = 1 CUP

METRIC TO US COOKING CONVERSIONS

OVEN TEMPERATURE

120℃ = 250° F

160℃ = 320° F

180℃ = 350° F

205℃ = 400° F

220℃ = 425° F

OVEN TEMPERATURE

8 FLUID OUNCES = 1 CUP = 1/2 PINT = 1/4 QUART

16 FLUID OUNCES = 2 CUPS = 1 PINT = 1/2 QUART

32 FLUID OUNCES = 4 CUPS = 2 PINTS = 1 QUART = 1/4 GALLON

128 FLUID OUNCES = 16 CUPS = 8 PINTS = 4 QUARTS = 1 GALLON

BAKING IN GRAMS

1 CUP FLOUR = 140 GRAMS

1 CUP SUGAR = 150 GRAMS

1 CUP POWDERED SUGAR = 160 GRAMS

1 CUP HEAVY CREAM = 235 GRAMS

VOLUME

1 MILLILITER = 1/5 TEASPOON

5 ML = 1 TEASPOON

15 ML = 1 TABLESPOON

240 ML = 1 CUP OR 8 FLUID OUNCES

1 LITER = 34 FL. OUNCES

WEIGHT

1 GRAM = .035 OUNCES

100 GRAMS = 3.5 OUNCES

500 GRAMS = 1.1 POUNDS

1 KILOGRAM = 35 OUNCES

US TO METRIC COOKING CONVERSIONS

1/5 TSP = 1 ML

1 TSP = 5 ML

1 TBSP = 15 ML

1 FL OUNCE = 30 ML

1 CUP = 237 ML

1 PINT (2 CUPS) = 473 ML

1 QUART (4 CUPS) = .95 LITER

1 GALLON (16 CUPS) = 3.8 LITERS

1 OZ = 28 GRAMS

1 POUND = 454 GRAMS

BUTTER

1 CUP BUTTER = 2 STICKS = 8 OUNCES = 230 GRAMS = 8 TABLESPOONS

BUTTER

1 CUP = 8 FLUID OUNCES

1 CUP = 16 TABLESPOONS

1 CUP = 48 TEASPOONS

1 CUP = 1/2 PINT

1 CUP = 1/4 QUART

1 CUP = 1/16 GALLON

1 CUP = 240 ML

BAKING PAN CONVERSIONS

1 CUP ALL-PURPOSE FLOUR = 4.5 OZ

1 CUP ROLLED OATS = 3 OZ 1 LARGE EGG = 1.7 OZ

1 CUP BUTTER = 8 OZ

1 CUP MILK = 8 OZ

1 CUP HEAVY CREAM = 8.4 OZ

1 CUP GRANULATED SUGAR = 7.1 OZ

1 CUP PACKED BROWN SUGAR = 7.75 OZ

1 CUP VEGETABLE OIL = 7.7 OZ

1 CUP UNSIFTED POWDERED SUGAR = 4.4 OZ

BAKING PAN CONVERSIONS

9-INCH ROUND CAKE PAN = 12 CUPS

10-INCH TUBE PAN =16 CUPS

11-INCH BUNDT PAN = 12 CUPS

9-INCH SPRINGFORM PAN = 10 CUPS

9 X 5 INCH LOAF PAN = 8 CUPS

9-INCH SQUARE PAN = 8 CUPS

Recipe for:

Ingredients:

Equipment:

Description:

Instructions:

Recipe

From the kicthen of ....

Serves .... Prep time .... Cook time ....

☐ Difficulty ☐ Easy ☐ Medium ☐ Hard

Ingredient

Directions

BBQ Grill & Smoker Cookbook

APPENDIX : RECIPES INDEX

A

Avocado Quesadillas 11

Apple And Walnut Muffins 18

Asian-inspired Broccoli 39

Apple-glazed Pork 59

Adobo Chicken 72

Apple, Peach, And Cranberry Crisp 96

B

Bread Pudding 11

Blueberry Dump Cake 15

Breakfast Chilaquiles 16

Banana Churros With Oatmeal 18

Bacon And Broccoli Bread Pudding 19

Breaded Green Olives 25

Blistered Lemony Green Beans 31

Bacon-wrapped Dates 34

Brussels Sprouts And Bacon 34

Bacon-wrapped Onion Rings And Spicy Aioli 35

Bean And Corn Stuffed Peppers 43

Black Bean And Tomato Chili 45

Bacon-wrapped Scallops 51

Bacon Burger Meatballs 54

Barbecue Pork Ribs 55

Balsamic Dressing 64

Buttermilk Ranch Chicken Tenders 69

Buttered Lobster Tails 82

Banana And Walnut Cake 88

Black And White Brownies 91

C

Cinnamon Toast With Strawberries 13

Cornflakes Toast Sticks 15

Coconut Brown Rice Porridge With Dates 16

Chocolate Banana Bread With White Chocolate 17

Cheesy Summer Squash With Red Onion 24

Cajun Zucchini Chips 26

Cheesy Apple Roll-ups 26

Cheesy Garlic Bread 26

Cheesy Crab Toasts 27

Cheesy Steak Fries 28

Cuban Sandwiches 30

Creamy Artichoke Dip With Pita Chips 32

Crispy Cod Fingers 33

Cheesy Asparagus And Potato Platter 37

Cheesy Broccoli Gratin 39

Crispy Noodle Vegetable Stir-fry 42

Crusted Brussels Sprouts With Sage 44

Cheesy Macaroni Balls 45

Corn Pakodas 47

Creamy Corn Casserole 47

Cashew Stuffed Mushrooms 48

Creamy And Cheesy Spinach 48

Cheesy Beef Meatballs 51

Carne Asada Tacos 53

Crispy Pork Tenderloin 53

Citrus Carnitas 57

Crackling Pork Roast 61

Creamy Ranch Dressing 63

Cashew Vodka Sauce 64

Cashew Pesto 65

Cashew Ranch Dressing 65

Chicken Cordon Bleu Roll-ups 70

Crispy Dill Pickle Chicken Wings 75

Crispy Chicken Parmigiana 77

Crispy Chicken Strips 77

Chili-lime Shrimp Skewers 79

Crab Cakes With Lemon-garlic Aioli 81

Crusted Codfish 81

Coconut Shrimp With Orange Chili Sauce 84

Chocolate Pecan Pie 88

Cinnamon Candied Apples 88

Chia Pudding 92

Churros With Chocolate-yogurt Sauce 95

Chocolate S'mores 97

Coffee Chocolate Cake 98

D

Deluxe Cheese Sandwiches 27

Dill Pickles 32

Deep Fried Duck Leg Quarters 71

E

Everything Bagel Breakfast Bake 13

Egg And Bacon Nests 16

English Pumpkin Egg Bake 22

Easy Beef Schnitzel 58

Everyday Cheesecake 90

Easy Blackberry Cobbler 94

F

Fluffy Pancake Sheet 22

French Fries 28

Flatbread Pizza 40

Fast And Easy Asparagus 44

Fresh Blueberry Cobbler 89

Fudge Pie 96

G

Grilled Breakfast Burritos 14

Grilled Sausage Mix 20

Garlic Fries 24

Grilled Carrots With Honey Glazed 25

Grilled Shishito Peppers 30

Grilled Vegetable Quesadillas 43

Garlic Roasted Asparagus 47

Grilled Mozzarella And Tomatoes 48

Garlic Herb Crusted Lamb 50

Grilled Pork Banh Mi 60

Golden Wasabi Spam 61

Garlic Lime Tahini Dressing 63

Ginger Sweet Sauce 63

Grilled Turkey Pesto Sandwiches 68

Ginger Chicken Thighs 70

Grilled Cornish Hens 75

Garlic Brown-butter Chicken With Tomatoes 76

Grilled Mahi-mahi Tacos With Spicy Coleslaw 80

Garlic Butter Shrimp Kebabs 82

Graham Cracker Cheesecake 92

H

Honey-lime Glazed Grilled Fruit Salad 22

Homemade Bbq Chicken Pizza 33

Honey-glazed Roasted Veggies 38

Honey-glazed Baby Carrots 40

Hearty Roasted Veggie Salad 46

Herb And Pesto Stuffed Pork Loin 54

Homemade Teriyaki Pork Ribs 56

Hummus 64

Honey-walnut Shrimp 80

Halibut With Lemon And Capers 85

I

Italian Sausage And Peppers 57

J

Jalapeño Poppers 34

L

Lush Vegetable Omelet 15

Loaded Zucchini Boats 40

Lamb Ribs With Fresh Mint 58

Lemon Dijon Vinaigrette 63

Lemon Parmesan Chicken 67

Lettuce Chicken Tacos With Peanut Sauce 73

Lime-garlic Grilled Chicken 74

Lemony Chicken And Veggie Kebabs 76

Lemon-garlic Butter Scallops 83

Lobster Rolls 83

Lemon Squares 90

Lemon Ricotta Cake 91

Lemony Blackberry Crisp 91

M

Maple Walnut Pancake 21

Mushroom And Spinach Calzones 29

Mozzarella Sticks 31

Mascarpone Mushrooms 41

Mozzarella Broccoli Calzones 41

Mozzarella Meatball Sandwiches With Basil 57

Marshmallow Banana Boat 92

N

Nut And Seed Muffins 17

O

Orange-ginger Soy Salmon 84

Orange Cake 95

P

Pesto Egg Croissantwiches 12

Pb&j 19

Potato Bread Rolls 20

Prosciutto Mini Mushroom Pizza 39

Pork Sausage With Cauliflower Mash 58

Pork Chops In Bourbon 60

Potato And Prosciutto Salad 61

Pico De Gallo 64

Pecan-crusted Turkey Cutlets 67

Pumpkin Pudding 94

Pound Cake With Mixed Berries 96

Peaches-and-cake Skewers 97

Q
Queso Bomb 30

R
Roasted Mixed Nuts 28

Rosemary Baked Cashews 33

Rack Of Lamb Chops With Rosemary 56

Rosemary Turkey Breast 74

Rum Grilled Pineapple Sundaes 94

Rich Chocolate Cookie 97

S
Sourdough Croutons 12

Stuffed Bell Peppers With Italian Maple-glazed Sausage 14

Soufflé 21

Sweet Potato Chips 27

Sausage And Mushroom Empanadas 29

Spicy Kale Chips 31

Stuffed Squash With Tomatoes And Poblano 37

Summer Squash And Zucchini Salad 38

Sriracha Golden Cauliflower 42

Spicy Cauliflower Roast 44

Simple Ratatouille 45

Spaghetti Squash Lasagna 50

Spicy Pork With Candy Onions 51

Spicy Beef Lettuce Wraps 52

Sweet And Tangy Beef 52

Smoked Beef 56

Salsa Verde Chicken Enchiladas 68

Sweet Chili Turkey Kebabs 69

Simple Whole Chicken Bake 71

Spicy Chicken Kebabs 73

Shrimp Boil 79

Striped Bass With Sesame-ginger Scallions 85

Sweet Potato Donuts 89

Strawberry Pizza 93

T
Twice Air-crisped Potatoes 35

Teriyaki Pork And Mushroom Rolls 55

Teriyaki Chicken And Bell Pepper Kebabs 71

Turkey Meatballs With Cranberry Sauce 72

Tilapia With Cilantro And Ginger 86

Tomato-stuffed Grilled Sole 86

U
Uncle's Famous Tri-tip 59

Ultimate Skillet Brownies 98

V
Veggie Frittata 12

Vegetarian Meatballs 46

Vietnamese Pork Chops 55

Vanilla Scones 93

Z
Zucchini And Potato Tots 25

Printed in Great Britain
by Amazon